Practice Finance
your questions answered

Second Edition

John Dean

*National Director of Accountancy Services
BMA Professional Services Ltd*

**provided as a service to the medical profession by
Astra Pharmaceuticals Ltd**

RADCLIFFE MEDICAL PRESS

© 1998 John Dean

Radcliffe Medical Press Ltd
18 Marcham Road, Abingdon, Oxon OX14 1AA, UK

First edition 1992

All rights reserved. No part of this publication may be reproduced, stored in a retrieval system, or transmitted, in any form or by any means, electronic, mechanical, photocopying, recording or otherwise without the prior permission of the copyright owner.

British Library Cataloguing in Publication Data

A catalogue record for this book is available from the British Library.

ISBN 1 85775 004 7

Library of Congress Cataloging-in-Publication Data is available.

Typeset by Advance Typesetting Ltd, Oxon
Printed and bound by Biddles Ltd, Guildford and King's Lynn

Contents

Preface		viii
1	**Financial Management and Accounts**	**1**
	1 Practice management	1
	2 Accounting records	2
	3 Bookkeeping	3
	4 Balancing the bank	5
	5 Petty cash control	7
	6 Leave advances	8
	7 Seniority and postgraduate education allowance	9
	8 Drawings calculations	10
	9 Stock on hand: dispensing practices	11
	10 Debtors in accounts	13
	11 Staff Christmas gifts	14
	12 Staffing budgets	15
2	**National Insurance**	**17**
	13 Classes of National Insurance	17
	14 Tax relief for National Insurance	18

3	**Organization and Collection of Tax**	19
15	Issue of tax demands	19
16	Interest on overdue tax	20
17	Interest on tax repayments	21
18	Allocation of tax repayments	21
19	Explanation of terms	23
20	Change to current year basis	24
21	Self-assessment for personal taxpayers	25
22	Self-assessment and partnerships	25
23	Penalties on non-submission of tax return	26
24	Trainee car allowance: taxation	27

4	**Partnerships in General Practice**	29
25	Income tax in partnerships	29
26	Allocation of assessable partnership profits	30
27	Introduction of capital	31
28	Relief for expenses on retirement	32
29	Progress to parity	33
30	New partners: additional income	34
31	Treatment of seniority awards etc.	35
32	Medical earnings: out of hours work	36
33	Accumulation of earnings in partnerships	37
34	Partnership deeds	38
35	De-merger of partnership	39
36	Taxation and drawings	39

5	**Surgeries and Cost-rents**	41
37	Surgery-related refunds	41
38	Notional rent assessment	42
39	Negative equity	43
40	Proceeds from surgery sale	44
41	Capital gains tax on surgery sale on retirement	45
42	Cost-rent income	46
43	Tax treatment of rent allowances	47
44	Allocation of rent allowances: partnerships	48
45	Rent and rates: health centres	48

	46	Rent payable by non-surgery-owning partners	50
	47	Abatement of direct refunds	51
	48	Income on surgery ownership after retirement	52
	49	Cost-rent finance	53
	50	Surgery: sole ownership	54
6	**Value Added Tax**		**55**
	51	VAT on new surgeries	55
	52	VAT: partial exemption scheme	56
7	**Practice Expenses**		**58**
	53	Practice expenses in partnerships	58
	54	'Duality of purpose'	59
	55	Child minding	60
	56	Claims for use of house	61
	57	Conference expenses	62
	58	Examination fees	63
	59	Video recorders	64
	60	Clothing	64
	61	Extra mortgage interest relief	65
	62	Sickness insurance premiums	66
8	**Cars and Travelling**		**67**
	63	Cars: time to purchase	67
	64	Financing car purchase	68
	65	Leasing cars	69
	66	Cars: capital allowances	69
	67	Expensive cars	70
	68	Trainee car allowance	70
	69	Mileage logs	72
9	**Capital Taxes**		**74**
	70	Capital Gains Tax on sale of shares	74
	71	Capital Gains Tax: annual exemption	75
	72	Inheritance Tax	76
	73	Inheritance Tax: surviving spouse exemption	77

		74 Tax on sale of land	77
		75 Capital Gains Tax on private house sale	78
10	**Wives, Spouses and Families**		**79**
		76 Married man's allowance	79
		77 Wife with outside employment	80
		78 Payment of wife's salary	81
		79 Married women doctors	82
		80 Wives' salaries in partnership	83
		81 Wives' pensions	84
		82 Medical insurance policies	85
		83 Tax in year of marriage	86
11	**Pensions, Superannuation and Retirement**		**87**
		84 24-hour retirement and abatement of pension	87
		85 Continuing superannuation contributions	88
		86 Tax allowance for superannuation	88
		87 Purchase of added years	90
		88 Private pension contributions: non-NHS income	91
		89 Renunciation of NHS tax relief	92
		90 Taxation of GP pension	93
		91 Cessation of practice: tax position	94
		92 Retirement from practice	95
		93 Retirement at 50	95
		94 Opting out of the NHS superannuation scheme	96
		95 Sale of surgery share on retirement	97
		96 Additional voluntary contributions	98
12	**Investments and Finance**		**100**
		97 Investments for children	100
		98 Tax-free investments	101
		99 PEPs	102
		100 Mid-term endowment policies	103
		101 Inheritance Tax exemption	103
		102 National Savings	104
		103 Saving through life assurance	105

13 Doctors and the Accountancy Profession — 107
- 104 Personal or partnership accountant? — 107
- 105 Accountancy fees — 108
- 106 Changing accountants — 109
- 107 Finding an accountant — 110
- 108 Bookkeeping — 111
- 109 Sources of information — 112

14 Practice Accounts — 113
- 110 Can I do it myself? — 113
- 111 Time taken to produce accounts — 114
- 112 Accounting year-ends — 115
- 113 Access to partnership accounts — 115
- 114 Changes in partnership — 116
- 115 Capital accounts — 117
- 116 Property capital accounts — 118
- 117 Property values — 119
- 118 Treatment of leave advances — 120
- 119 Accruals: basis of accounts — 121
- 120 Partnerships: treatment of target payments — 123
- 121 Adjustments to partners' balances — 123
- 122 'Grossing-up' — 124
- 123 Cash flow — 125

15 GP Fundholding — 129
- 124 Professional assistance — 129
- 125 Audit of accounts — 130
- 126 Fundholding bank account — 131
- 127 Bank interest and charges — 132
- 128 Interest on fundholding bank account — 132
- 129 Fund savings: how to spend them — 133
- 130 Fund savings: ownership by partners — 134
- 131 Surplus invested in surgery — 135
- 132 Savings in ancillary staff costs — 136
- 133 GP fundholding taxation — 136

Index — 139

Preface

Doctors are great askers of questions. There is nothing wrong with this, but the professional who seeks to advise GPs on their finances should find that such questions hold out no great horrors for him and he should be perfectly capable of answering them.

In many years practising as an accountant to GPs I have been asked all the questions that appear in this book, and many more which are too numerous to cover. GPs' questions invariably fall into several categories; it is quite evident that the question of arrangements for the taxation of partnerships, particularly relating to the allocations of taxation assessments, is one that causes great problems and which I have tried to deal with as fully as possible. This will be further emphasized when the arrangements for new systems of taxing practice profits come into force.

Many doctors are concerned about the arrangements for their retirement income. Those doctors who own surgeries are extremely concerned about such matters as how to finance partnership changes and particularly how they can realize their capital in the surgery on retirement. Also, there is great concern about eligibility for Capital Gains Tax retirement relief. All these are dealt with in the text.

In preparing this book every effort has been made to keep it as up-to-date as possible. Taxation questions in particular take into account all known legislation up to and including the March 1998 Budget and the 1998 Review Body report. However, where interest rates are shown, the reader should bear in mind that while correct at the time of preparation they can, and do, change at fairly frequent intervals. No decisions based upon these should be taken without obtaining up-to-date advice.

In 1996/97, there came into force the biggest change we have seen in our lifetime in the manner in which personal taxation is administered. The self-assessment rules, which now put the ultimate responsibility on the taxpayer for the filing of his returns in good time, subject to fairly stringent penalties, largely involve the submission of returns by 31 January 1998 (shortly before publication of this edition). It remains to be seen how many GPs have fallen foul of the rules and whose returns were not submitted in time.

I should like to acknowledge the assistance I have received from a number of professional colleagues in dealing with and reviewing certain of the questions in the book. In particular, my colleague, Jackie Roberts, has assisted me in reviewing the section on GP fundholding. Any errors are, however, mine alone.

It has become apparent since this book was first issued in mid-1992 that GPs, who have had the good sense to acquire it in satisfactorily large numbers, appreciate the presentation of financial facts in this form. This second edition, now published over five years later, will help, not only to satisfy GPs' thirst for knowledge in this ever-changing field, but will also cover those new factors which have emerged since the first edition was published.

John Dean
March 1998

Note: Although it is manifestly not the case, it has been assumed throughout that GPs are male and all the practice managers are female. This is purely in the interests of brevity, and no other interpretation should be placed upon it.

1

Financial Management and Accounts

▲ Question 1: Practice management

I am a junior partner in a practice of six doctors. For some time I have felt concerned about the management of the practice although I am reluctant to raise this with my senior partners, who seem quite happy to go along with the situation. However, I feel it is affecting the efficiency of the practice and that we are not so profitable as we might be.

The senior partner insists on doing all the practice accounting himself; there is no-one to submit claims to the Health Authority (HA) and I have no idea how my drawings are calculated. I would like us to recruit a practice manager to do this work but my partners tell me it will be too expensive. Should I raise this with them or look for another practice that is more attuned to my ideals?

Undoubtedly, you require the services of an experienced practice manager, who could take away from the doctors the whole of the administrative function of the practice, dealing with such matters as practice accountancy, submission of claims, organization of rotas, calculations of drawings, and so on. Such an individual may be expensive but you are likely to be able to obtain a substantial contribution towards her salary and almost certainly she would, by increased efficiency, earn for the practice much more than her residual salary cost. In view of present cash-limiting policies, it would be as well to check with your HA the amount of refund you are likely to attract.

It is not good practice for routine bookkeeping work to be done by doctors as it can be done by a practice manager or bookkeeper appointed specifically for that purpose. With a practice of your size, it may be that you could engage a part-time bookkeeper who would be responsible to the practice manager.

Only you can decide whether it is politic to raise this with your partners, but it may help if you could recruit at least one other partner to your point of view, or you might feel able to persuade the partners to listen to the point of view of a respected outsider, such as the practice accountant, banker or solicitor, who is likely to be sympathetic to your views.

Partners should always voice their concerns. They are remunerated by sharing the practice profits and therefore all partners must feel involved, both in the management of the practice and the decision-making process.

▲ Question 2: Accounting records

I am a GP in practice and I have been told I should keep proper books of account. I have never kept books before. Can you tell me what advantages there would be in doing so? Can my accountant do it?

There are many advantages in keeping proper books of account. You have not said whether you are in sole practice or partnership but if you are in a partnership you should have proper accounts. This will enable the partners to see that their earnings are calculated correctly in accordance with profit-sharing ratios, that they are drawing out sufficient funds from the account and to preserve equity between them.

Apart from this, and regardless of your type of practice, properly kept books of account will enable you to ensure that all amounts earned are paid into your bank account and that all cheques are properly drawn. It will be easier and less expensive for your accountant to draw up final accounts at your year-end and will enable you to keep a constant check on the cumulative expenditure in any given period.

It is extremely irresponsible for medical practices, some of which are extremely large and thriving businesses in their own right, not to keep properly written-up books of account. Ideally, the work should be delegated to a properly qualified practice manager or, in the larger practices, to a specialist bookkeeper employed for the purpose. A well drawn-up partnership deed is also likely to include a provision that proper accounting records be kept.

In addition, new rules introduced with the advent of tax self-assessment mean that those in business (including GPs) can be heavily penalized where proper account books cannot be supplied to the Inland Revenue on request.

In many cases, practices which cannot keep proper books may have them written up by their accountant, again at considerably more expense. If you employ a member of your staff to do this work, you will receive an element of reimbursement of their salary. You will only receive tax relief on your accountant's fees and would pay 17.5% VAT on top of his charges.

▲ Question 3: Bookkeeping

I am advised, and accept, that I should keep account books. I know nothing whatever about bookkeeping and should like to know exactly what books I should keep. I cannot afford to pay a bookkeeper and will have to do the work myself.

The books you keep, broadly speaking, should consist of: (a) a main cash book, which should be regularly updated and reconciled to your practice bank account; (b) a petty cash book for recording sundry small outgoings; (c) a cash received book for recording sundry cash fees, certificate monies, cremation fees and so on, which should be paid into the bank at regular intervals; (d) a salaries book to record payments and deductions for your employees; and (e) if appropriate, a ledger to record work for private patients and to enable you to check whether their bills have been settled. Also, a Health Authority (HA) income analysis book provides a useful breakdown of NHS income and enables you to both control and monitor earnings from this source.

This is a fairly basic system; it may be that in some practices more complete systems will be required and special advice should be obtained about this.

There is now an increasing trend towards computerization in medical practices and some practices are providing computerized accounting records for their own in-house facility. This should not be introduced, however, without ensuring, with your professional advisers, that the program to be used is specifically tailored for use in medical practices, where accounting requirements are likely to be very different from those in more conventional businesses. Ensure also that the analysis headings to be used are compatible with the requirements of your own practice.

Who you get to do the work is up to you. I doubt, however, whether you will be happy spending a fair bit of time writing up your account books each week – or more frequently – after a busy day at the surgery. You would be well advised to engage the services of a competent bookkeeper, who may not necessarily have to work more than, say, half a day a week and would be relatively inexpensive.

▲ Question 4: Balancing the bank

I am trying to install a practice bookkeeping system and have been told that I should reconcile and balance the bank account regularly. What does this mean and why should I do it?

It is indeed essential to balance your main cash book and reconcile this to your bank account at regular intervals. This should be done as a double check, to ensure your cash books are properly and accurately maintained, and that your bank is properly recording your transactions. In addition, it enables you to check which cheques you have issued have not been presented for payment and these can, if necessary, be re-issued. The trend towards direct debits and credits means that such entries must be ascertained from the bank statement and corresponding entries made in the cash book.

The process of reconciling the bank account is normally done monthly and should commence with a brief statement starting with the balance on hand shown on your bank statement at the end of a given month (say 30 June). This balance should then be adjusted, by additions for amounts paid to the bank but not yet credited on the bank statement; and by deductions for cheques you have issued but which have not as yet been presented at the bank for payment. If your cash book has been properly written up and everything else is in order, the product of this statement should then balance with the difference between the receipts and payments side in your cash book, after taking into consideration the opening balance at the start of the period.

If it does not balance, steps should be taken to see that it does. Remember that it is far easier to trace a difference over a period of say a month, than over a full year, during which time numerous transactions will have taken place and the procedure will consequently be far more time-consuming. It would be even more time-consuming and expensive if this statement had to be prepared by your accountant, who would obviously charge a fee for doing the work. If you are a large practice with many transactions, this could well take him several days to complete and he would base his charge on the hours taken to do the work. A typical bank reconciliation statement is shown in Figure 1.

```
DRS BLACK, WHITE, GREEN, ORANGE AND BLUE

BANK RECONCILIATION STATEMENT AS AT 30 JUNE 1998
                                              £              £
Balance as per Bank Statement (No. 245)                  20 531.28
Add: Late credits                          783.45
                                           289.78
                                                          1 073.23
                                                         21 604.51

Less: Unpresented cheques
No.  927                                    24.68
     042                                   344.97
     043                                   248.23
     045                                   492.78
     049                                   395.84
     050                                    42.75
     051                                   849.86
     053                                   346.94
     054                                 3 429.00
     055                                 4 276.00
     056                                 3 087.00
     057                                 2 275.00
     058                                 1 896.00
                                                         17 709.05
Balance as per Cash Book                                  3 895.46
```

Figure 1: Illustration showing the agreement of a typical bank account at 30 June 1998. It will be seen that the balance shown on the bank statement (£20 531.28) is very different from the true balance (£3 895.46) shown in the cash book and why it is important to be aware of the true balance at all times.

▲ Question 5: Petty cash control

My practice occasionally receives money in respect of sundry fees taken at the reception desk for certificates, various examinations that are paid for by patients, and so on. We have been using these funds for paying out small expenditure such as cleaners' wages, postage stamps, etc. and dividing the balance between the partners at any date. None of this has passed through our accounts. I am told that this is wrong. Is this the case and how should it be corrected?

It most certainly is wrong. If unrecorded fees have been received over a lengthy period and paid directly to the partners without passing through the accounts, there is a danger that if HM Inspector of Taxes finds out he could raise an in-depth enquiry into the receipt of these fees for several back years and you could be liable for heavy interest and penalties, based upon the tax lost to the Inland Revenue. Bear in mind that if this actual petty cash expenditure had been fully and properly recorded it would have been eligible for perfectly legitimate tax relief. There are also likely to be PAYE complications if wages paid to cleaners have not properly passed through the PAYE system.

You would be well advised to discuss this problem with your accountant and make a full disclosure to the Inland Revenue, which is a far less painful exercise than if the Inland Revenue discover this on their own and have to drag the information out of you.

Apart from this, it is strongly advised that you collect these cash fees together, in a tin specially maintained for the purpose, these also being recorded at the same time in a special account book. At either a fixed period, say weekly, or when the amount in the tin has reached, say £50, this should then be paid into the practice bank account as part of the partnership income.

You will undoubtedly require funds from time to time from which to defray sundry small cash items and it is suggested this is done by drawing a float from the bank at fixed times, probably monthly depending on the circumstances, out of which these payments can be made. Again, these payments should be specially recorded in a petty cash book, which should be balanced monthly and the balance in hand carried forward from month to month.

▲ Question 6: Leave advances

I understand there is a scheme for borrowing money from the NHS in order to pay for one's holiday. Is this right and how do I go about it? Is this money taxable?

You are talking here about the leave advance, which is an advance of 20% of the basic practice allowance (BPA) currently in force. The 1998/99 rate of BPA is £7776, so that a GP who submits a claim for the leave advance on form FP75 by 15 April 1998 will be entitled to an advance of 20% of that, or £1555.20. Some HAs round this figure up or down to the nearest pound.

It is likely to be necessary for you to justify your claim on the grounds that you will actually take some element of leave at the time the advance is required.

This advance is repaid by equal quarterly instalments by deduction on your quarterly HA statement, so that the whole of the amount is recovered by 31 March in the year following the advance. Detailed conditions are set out in SFA paragraph 12.15.

You have not received any more income than you would otherwise do but have merely drawn it out a little earlier. The leave advance in itself is not therefore taxable.

▲ Question 7: Seniority and postgraduate education allowance

I recently joined my practice as a partner. I received a postgraduate education allowance as I qualify for this by having attended the required number of lectures.

I find, however, that this is not being paid to me. As I have qualified for this, is it not right and proper that I should receive credit for it?

This really all depends on the policy of the particular partnership. It is not a question of what is right and what is wrong, but whether the same policy applies to all the partners. What would be eminently wrong, however, would be if the other partners were to receive their shares of seniority/PGEA and you were not to receive yours.

The policy of each partnership in this connection should be clearly set down in the partnership deed. If there is no deed in existence (*see* Question 34) then you should have received on appointment a letter of engagement which would set down clearly the terms under which you were to be remunerated.

It is suggested that you check with the practice manager, or whoever calculates the drawings, to see why this has occurred. If necessary, raise the matter with the senior partner. If a partnership deed is in existence and you have signed it, refer to the appropriate section in the deed.

If you are unable to solve this through partnership discussion, very much as a last resort and provided you are a member, you may like to consult the BMA Conciliation Service which may also be able to help in this matter.

▲ Question 8: Drawings calculations

I am a partner in a practice of six. We pay ourselves an amount each month that I have always regarded as a salary but now I am told that it is not, and that it could go down as well as up. I always thought that my income was geared to the annual review body award. Is this not right? How should my monthly payment be calculated?

GPs are self-employed principals in their practices and are not salaried employees. The money you are paid each month therefore is not a salary, as would be the case if you were, say, a hospital doctor, but it is merely a payment to you on account of your profits, which cannot exactly be quantified until your annual accounts are prepared each year. In this respect, you are no different from any other self-employed businessman.

It is normal for such monthly drawings to be calculated by taking into account all known factors such as income tax payments, superannuation, added years contributions, seniority awards and numerous other matters. If this is not done properly and accurately it will inevitably have an effect on your current account balance each year and it will be necessary for this to be equalized. If you have been overpaid you may well be asked to make a refund to the practice so that it is essential that an accurate and systematic method of paying monthly amounts to you and your partners is in force.

There are numerous methods by which drawings can be calculated. Many practices which prefer to have a regular payment each month choose to implement a regular drawings system, by which either the practice or the accountant calculates the likely profits for the coming year, makes all necessary adjustments as indicated above and reduces this to an equal monthly payment. While these cannot be entirely accurate, many practices prefer them for reasons of confidence and security.

Some other practices prefer to calculate their drawings more exactly on a monthly and quarterly basis, taking into consideration all known variations at those dates. This is probably the most accurate method available, provided that it can be done within the practice, by either the practice manager or the financial partner. However, the variable and uncertain levels of monthly drawings can cause personal financial difficulties for younger partners.

It cannot be emphasized too strongly how necessary it is for such drawings to be calculated efficiently as indicated above. If you have problems you should seek advice from your accountant who should be able to advise you on drawings systems of this nature.

A typical calculation of regular monthly drawings is shown in Figure 2 (*see* page 12).

▲ Question 9: Stock on hand: dispensing practices

I am a partner in a dispensing practice. We have never valued our stock of drugs on hand, except at infrequent partnership changes that have never coincided with our accounting year-end. We make our accounts up to 31 December each year.

We recently changed our accountant and our new accountant now tells us that we should count the stock and value it at each 31 December, is this correct?

Your accountant is perfectly correct in advising you that you should value your stock. If you do not do so your accounts will almost certainly show an incorrect calculation of the profits earned by the partnership during the year from your dispensing operation. This could well result in you paying more or less tax than your correct liability.

Apart from this, the Inspector of Taxes would be quite within his rights in insisting that a correct and accurate value of the stock is included in the accounts each year. If this is not done he could well raise assessments on tax theoretically lost in previous years due to the non-inclusion of this stock. This procedure could prove

CALCULATION OF REGULAR DRAWINGS YEAR 1997/98
(TO MARCH 1998)

	Total	Dr A (28%)	Dr B (28%)	Dr C (24%)	Dr D (20%)
Estimated partnership profits for year	90 000	25 200	25 200	21 600	18 000
Seniority awards	5 900	3 900	2 000	–	–
Postgraduate education allowance	1 500	–	–	–	1 500
Total income (estimated) (1)	97 400	29 100	27 200	21 600	19 500
Deductions:					
Superannuation (estimated)	5 600	1 600	1 500	1 300	1 200
Added years	1 300	800	300	200	–
On outside appointments (estimated)	100	–	20	80	–
National Insurance (estimated):					
Class 1 (appointments)	100	–	–	100	–
Class 2 (stamps)	960	240	240	240	240
Repayment of leave advance	4 824	1 206	1 206	1 206	1 206
Repayment of loans (GPFC)	1 300	–	–	500	800
	14 184	3 846	3 266	3 626	3 446
Income tax reserve transfers:					
1997/98	18 000	6 500	5 500	4 000	2 000
Total outgoings (2)	32 184	10 346	8 766	7 626	5 446
Net (1–2)	65 216	18 754	18 434	13 974	14 054
Monthly (÷ 12)	5 434	1 563	1 536	1 164	1 171
(But say) …	5 400	1 550	1 500	1 150	1 150

Figure 2: A typical calculation of regular monthly drawings in a practice. Values used are for illustration purposes only and are somewhat below intended remuneration levels. The details of likely items to be adjusted on periodic drawings calculations are: 1. *Income* – (a) Seniority awards, (b) Postgraduate education allowances, and (c) Notional cost-rent allowances (where to be distributed in different ratios to partnership shares); 2. *Outgoings* – (a) Superannuation contributions: standard, (b) Added years/unreduced lump sum, (c) National Insurance contributions, (d) Repayment of leave advances, (e) GPFC (or other) loan repayments and interest, and (f) Transfers to Income Tax reserve.

expensive in terms of repayment of lost tax, interest and possible penalties. In an extreme case, you could find yourself paying tax properly incurred by partners who have subsequently left the practice.

For all these reasons, the inclusion of an accurate figure of stock of dispensing drugs on hand is essential each year for dispensing practices. In practice, this work would probably be carried out by your own staff. Alternatively, you could engage a professional valuer but should check the level of his fee beforehand. Do not forget to add VAT to the actual stock value. Stock received as free samples should be excluded.

▲ Question 10: Debtors in accounts

We have recently received the accounts of my practice and I took them to a friend who is a specialist accountant and asked him to look at them. Somewhat to my dismay he pointed out that there was virtually nothing in these accounts (only about £50) in respect of debtors. What does this mean and why should the debtors be larger?

Debtors are amounts due to the practice (or any other business) at any given date. If, for instance, your practice makes up its accounts to 31 March annually and on 15 March you perform a service for a private patient, issue an invoice for £100 which is not paid until 15 April, then at the end of your accounting year that amount is a debtor and must be brought into the accounts as such.

That is a relatively simple example but the principle also extends to NHS incomes, some of which are paid several months in arrear, as well as to the various refunds which are due at any given date. For instance, in dispensing practices, the drug refunds are often not made until three months after the month of prescribing, item of service fees are frequently paid up to a quarter in arrears, whilst health promotion payments are invariably paid during the first few days of the succeeding month. Your accounts are likely to be prepared on the income and expenditure – rather than receipt and payments – basis and must reflect your actual earnings during the year, regardless of when these are received.

It is therefore essential for these debtors to be brought into the accounts. Whilst no hard and fast rules can be given, it is common practice in a properly drawn-up set of accounts to see a figure of debtors running into several tens of thousands of pounds.

▲ Question 11: Staff Christmas gifts

I am a GP in a partnership and at Christmas we have been used to paying cash gifts to our staff. We are now told by our accountant that this must cease. Surely we can make a Christmas gift to our staff?

You may well have misunderstood what your accountant advised. Neither he nor anyone else can stop you making Christmas gifts to your staff if you wish, but there are certain taxation implications arising from these gifts of which you should be aware and which may affect your decision.

If you make the gifts out of your own pockets, purely as a personal gift, and these do not pass through the partnership accounts, you will be unable to claim tax relief on the payments yourselves. The recipients could still find themselves liable for tax and National Insurance contributions (NIC) if, as is likely to be the case, the relationship between you is purely of a business nature.

If, however, the doctors wish to include these in their accounts in order to claim tax relief, it must be accepted that the recipients will be taxed on them. If the gift is of money or money's worth, which includes various types of tokens and vouchers, the amounts should be entered on the tax deduction cards of the employees concerned, with tax and NIC being deducted as required.

Until recently, it was assumed that no tax would be chargeable on gifts in kind; goods, foodstuffs, drinks and so on, which cannot readily be converted into cash. A recent ruling of the Inland Revenue, however, means that this is not the case. If gifts in kind are made to higher-paid employees (in tax law those earning over £8500 p.a. including benefits) they are chargeable in full to tax on the cost of the gift to the employer. In the case of lower-paid employees, that is, those earning less than that amount, they are chargeable to tax on the assumed second-hand value of the goods concerned. Ideally, gifts of this nature should be reported to the Inland Revenue at the end of the tax year concerned, giving the values involved, so that assessments can be raised on those employees if necessary.

Another option available to the employer is to make a gift of such an amount as, after deduction of tax and NIC, will leave a balance due to the employee of the amount the employer wishes to donate. This will, of course, be more expensive to the employer.

If you spend money on a Christmas party for your staff, above a certain level, the employee can also be liable for tax.

▲ Question 12: Staffing budgets

My practice obtains a refund of our ancillary staff salaries, but when we see our annual accounts we find that the recovery rate falls from year to year. Last year it was about 68%. This year (year to 31 December 1997) it has fallen to about 59%. Can you suggest any reason for this and how we can correct it?

These days, although practice does vary between different Health Authorities, in the majority of cases practices are given an annual budget which they must work to in order to ensure that staffing levels are correct and that their recovery rate is realistic.

Thus, if a practice were to be given, say, an annual staffing budget of £140 000, then this would represent 70% of £200 000. Ideally, you should also receive 100% recovery of your staff National Insurance contributions.

What may well have happened in your own practice is that staffing levels have been allowed to run out of hand and that your wage bill is well above the maximum. You would be well advised to consider staffing levels very carefully; consider the salaries you are paying and try and equate this with the potential recovery which should be known at the start of each year. An efficient budgeting process should help you in achieving this.

2

National Insurance

▲ Question 13: Classes of National Insurance

I have recently joined a practice as a partner, after some years in hospital service and as a GP trainee. I understand that I might now have to pay National Insurance at a different rate and wonder if you can advise me how much this will be?

Class 2 National Insurance is paid either by direct debit or by a system of quarterly accounts which will be sent to you by the Contributions Agency, who are the authority responsible for collecting National Insurance contributions (NICs). For the year 1998/99, these Class 2 NI contributions will be levied at the rate of £6.35 a week.

Many young doctors join practices, having previously paid Class 1 contributions from their salary. If they do nothing about it, it may well be years before the National Insurance authorities discover that they have not paid their correct level of contributions, when a large sum in arrears will become payable. It is best to avoid this situation at all costs.

You would therefore be strongly advised to contact the Contributions Agency, Class 2 Group, DSS, Longbenton, Newcastle Upon Tyne NE98 1YX. Tel: 0191 225 6762. They will advise you how much is payable and confirm whether you wish to pay your contributions by direct debit or quarterly account.

You will also be liable to Class 4, earnings-related contributions. These are paid with your normal half-yearly income tax demand (*see* Question 15). These are, for 1998/99, at the rate of 6% on a band of income between £7310 and £25 220 per annum. This band is charged at 6%, giving a maximum contribution for the 1998/99 year of £1074.60. Most GPs earning taxable income in excess of £25 220 per annum will therefore find that their Class 2 contribution for the present year is of that amount. They will find that one-half is included with their half-yearly tax demand.

▲ Question 14: Tax relief for National Insurance

Can I get any income tax relief on my National Insurance contributions?

You can only get direct relief for National Insurance contributions (NICs) paid on behalf of employees. If you are a GP in practice and pay Class 1 NICs on your ancillary staff, you will find that the employer's share of these is likely to be refunded in full by the HA, so that in effect this will cancel out any relief you might have obtained on the payments. It is of course, infinitely preferable to have the whole of the contribution refunded, than to merely obtain income tax relief at a rate no higher than 40%!

If you pay Class 1 contributions for any employees who are non-qualifying ancillary staff (such as cleaners or employed doctors), and you can clearly show that they are genuine employees in practice, you will obtain tax relief on both the employer's and employee's share, where the latter is deducted from the gross salary paid to the employee.

There is no tax relief whatever on the Class 2 and Class 4 contributions paid by GPs.

3

Organization and Collection of Tax

▲ Question 15: Issue of tax demands

I find that I regularly get income tax demands that mystify and disturb me considerably as they are much greater than the income I actually earn. Usually my accountant writes later and tells me that the amount of tax is not due; nevertheless I cannot understand why I get these large demands in the first place.

The reason why you have been sent estimated – and probably excessive – tax demands is that if he does not know the amount of your income for a given year, the Inspector of Taxes will issue an estimated assessment on those profits. The responsibility has then been on you to appeal against these assessments within a period of 30 days.

Your accountant, who may or may not be responsible for the non-submission of accounts in the first place, has nevertheless done his job properly by appealing against the assessments and recommending what he feels to be reasonable amounts of tax to pay.

This system has in effect now ceased. No tax assessments for sole practitioners will have been issued since 1995/96, and in respect of partnerships the last year was 1996/97. This is due to the new system of self-assessment which has now been brought into force (*see* Question 21).

▲ Question 16: Interest on overdue tax

I understand that if I owe tax to the Inland Revenue they can charge me interest on this. Is this correct and when will I have to pay it? Is it worth my while delaying my income tax payment and paying interest?

There is indeed a charge for interest on unpaid tax, which counts from the due date. At the time of writing, the interest charge is 9.5%, which is not tax-deductible. Therefore it is almost certainly worth your while to pay your tax on the due date and not incur any interest charges.

Interest normally commences on the date the tax falls due for payment. In any event, the Inland Revenue will not wait for ever for their money. Successive and ever more threatening demands will be raised, with ultimate legal action being taken to enforce payment.

You would be well advised to operate some scheme of setting funds aside out of which tax liabilities can be paid *as and when* they fall due.

▲ Question 17: Interest on tax repayments

If I have a repayment of income tax due to me by the Inland Revenue, will they pay me interest if the amount due is delayed?

Yes, they will pay you interest but, as with most of these rules, this works very much in favour of the Inland Revenue.

Unlike the conditions for payment of interest on overdue tax (*see* Question 16), the interest (officially known as the repayment supplement) on tax repayments only runs from one year after the end of the year of assessment concerned. Therefore, if you were to have an income tax repayment, say, for the year 1996/97, interest would not commence to run until one year afterwards, in other words from 6 April 1998. However, this is perhaps not so unfair as it sounds; in the case of a Schedule D tax payment, the second instalment of tax for that year would not have been paid until 3 months after the end of the year of assessment, that is, on 31 July 1997.

Certainly, the Inland Revenue would have the use of your money, free of interest for this period, which can really only be avoided by dealing properly with tax assessments, appeals and payment of a realistic amount of tax until this can be accurately calculated.

At the time of writing, the rate of interest is 4.5%.

▲ Question 18: Allocation of tax repayments

My practice has just received a large income tax repayment of about £5000, covering several years. We are a six-partner practice and the partners all have different tax liabilities, due to different allowances and reliefs, loan interest, and so on.

I cannot see how this tax repayment has been divided between the partners and, when enquiring from our accountants, I was told it had been divided in profit-sharing ratios. Surely this is wrong? How should the interest be treated that was paid to us with the repayment and how is this calculated?

To take the latter item first, interest on income tax repayments (officially known as the repayment supplement) runs at a prescribed rate of interest from one year after the year of assessment. Therefore, if you are due a repayment for the year 1995/96, interest would not commence to run until 6 April 1997.

With regard to the income tax repayment you have received, this should be allocated between the partners by comparing each partner's respective tax liability with the amount you have already paid on account for that year. Therefore, if say for the 1995/96 year the total partnership tax liability was £20 000, and you have paid £25 000 on account, you will get a repayment of £5000. It is, however, highly unlikely that this will be divided equally between the partners or in their profit-sharing ratios. Of that £25 000 paid, let us say that one partner has paid £6000. If it ultimately emerges that his true liability is £5250, he will be due a repayment of £750, together with any proportionate interest that might have accrued. On the same basis, other partners may well be due a much higher repayment or may even have a shortfall in liability and be asked to pay more.

All these figures should be available in the papers of your accountant who should be able to advise you exactly how they are arrived at and how the liability is divided between the partners. This has nothing whatever to do with your profit-sharing ratios and most certainly the repayment should not be divided in that way.

▲ Question 19: Explanation of terms

I cannot understand various terms used in connection with my accounts and tax. I usually tell my accountant all details of my car expenses and other items but these are never entered on my income tax return. My accountant prepares a set of accounts for my partnership for me each year. I thought this was my income tax return.

No, it is not! You are confusing what are in fact three very separate items, each of which, if they are not given their proper name, will be bound to cause constant misunderstanding and confusion.

Your income tax return is a printed form that is issued by Her Majesty's Inspector of Taxes each year to all Schedule D taxpayers throughout the country. This is normally printed with the year of assessment at the top and will bear the name of the taxpayer. This will be the means by which you return to the Inland Revenue all details of personal income and reliefs, such as any income from deposit accounts or dividends, claiming relief for interest payments, and so on, and is completed for a fiscal year ending on 5 April.

The other document you are thinking of is your annual claim for personal practice expenses. As you are a partner, this will usually consist of items that you pay for personally and claim outside the medium of your partnership accounts. It will normally be made up to the same year-end as you prepare your partnership accounts. (*See* Question 53.)

The other items to which you refer are your practice or partnership accounts. These are made up to a year-end, which is entirely your own choice (*see* Question 112), although once decided it is unlikely there will be any change. These accounts will show the profit made by your practice or partnership for the year and are the basis upon which assessments to income tax are made.

These three documents are quite different and must be called by their proper names if confusion is to be avoided.

▲ Question 20: Change to current year basis

I have been in practice for many years as a sole practitioner, making up my accounts to 30 September annually. My accountant tells me that I will have to pay tax a year earlier in the future. Is this correct and will I have to pay two years' tax in one?

First, to set one point at rest. What you are talking about is the change from the preceding year to the current year basis of assessment. It is true that there is an 'overlapping' year during this change but this is catered for by the transitional arrangements (*see* below) and there is no prospect of you having to pay tax twice in any given year.

Under the new current year basis, what this really means is that instead of paying tax up to two years after you earn the profits you will pay it, chiefly, about one year afterwards. This is in reality no more than a cash flow problem and will effectively only represent an increased outgoing where profits are rising at a rate above average. You will certainly not have to pay two lots of tax in one year.

For a practice such as your own which makes up its accounts to 30 September each year, your accounts to 30 September 1994, which formed the basis of assessment to tax in 1995/96, were the last to be assessed under the preceding year basis.

The first year for which the current year basis applies fully is 1997/98, when you are taxed on the basis of profits earned in the year to 30 September 1997. It follows that there are two years which have not apparently been taxed: those to 30 September 1995 and 30 September 1996. These two years are taken and averaged together so that you effectively pay tax in 1996/97 on half the profits generated in the two-year period.

It will be seen that by this process a year's profits have effectively dropped out of charge to tax.

▲ Question 21: Self-assessment for personal taxpayers

I understand that I will have to work out my own tax in future. This has always been done by the Inspector of Taxes and my accountant. Will I now have to do it all myself or can my accountant help me?

You appear to be slightly confusing some of the potential effects of the change to self-assessment for personal taxpayers. There is no reason whatever why you should not continue to use your accountant to settle your tax liabilities with the Revenue and, indeed, the vast majority of GPs will do so.

The major difference is that the essential working out of the necessary figures will be done by the taxpayer or his accountant, rather than by the Inspector of Taxes. Attached to each personal income tax return will be a schedule from which it is possible to work out one's annual tax liability and this return must be submitted to the Revenue at the proper time with a cheque for the amount outstanding.

▲ Question 22: Self-assessment and partnerships

We have always been used to paying our tax as a partnership, with each partner reserving an amount each month so that the full amount is available when the tax falls due for settlement.

I understand that this system has now ceased. Is this correct and how shall we pay our tax in the future?

Up to 1996/97, income tax assessments have been issued in the name of partnerships. If, therefore, we have a practice of four doctors, Doctors A, B, C and D, that is the name in which the tax assessment was issued rather than in the name of the individual doctors. Perhaps more importantly, in law partners are jointly and severally liable for the debts of the partnership. For this purpose income tax is a debt due by the partnership and if a partner for some reason defaults on his payment or cannot be found at the proper time, then the liability falls back on the other partners.

Under the self-assessment arrangements, this no longer applies; each individual partner is treated separately and will be assumed by the Revenue to be running a small practice of his own. The tax will be demanded separately from that particular doctor and he alone will be liable for it. Partners will no longer have a potential liability for the tax debts of their partners.

Those partners who have been used to setting aside money in a separate bank account out of which these tax liabilities can be paid should question whether they propose to do so in the future. In many cases partnerships will find it convenient to do so for cash flow purposes and will wish to continue the present system.

▲ Question 23: Penalties on non-submission of tax return

I understand that I can be fined if I do not send my tax return in at the proper time. In the past I have not been very good at getting the figures ready for my tax return, which my accountant tells me is fairly complex. What will happen to me if I do not do this in the future. Will I be prosecuted?

It is highly unlikely that you will be prosecuted through the Courts unless the situation gets entirely out of hand.

Under the new regime, those taxpayers who wish the Revenue to work out their liability must submit their returns by 30 September following the year to which the return relates. If the tax is to be worked out by the taxpayer (or his advisor) then the return must be submitted by 31 January. If the return is not in by that date then the taxpayer will incur a penalty of £100; the penalties follow an increasing scale thereafter.

To complete and submit a tax return within a period of ten months is by no means unduly onerous and it is suggested that those GPs who have not felt able to do so in the past should do their utmost to ensure they are submitted on time. Failure to do so could be extremely expensive.

▲ Question 24: Trainee car allowance: taxation

We have recently become a training practice. Our new GP registrar has insisted that we pay his car allowance to him free of tax, not including this with taxable pay from which the monthly PAYE tax is calculated. Is this correct, and has he any right to insist that this is not taxed? We are not anxious to involve the practice in an expensive tax liability.

You are quite right to be cautious: the registrar has no right whatsoever to insist that his car allowance is not taxed. Some practices in recent years have, in fact, been charged arrears of tax by the Inland Revenue, as the practice (as the employer) is liable for the tax that they should have deducted from the trainee car allowance but did not.

It is also fair to say that, for many years, tax offices turned a blind eye to this, being quite content to allow it to remain untaxed under the assumption that the relief would be recovered by motoring expenses. Since then, however, the attitude of the Inland Revenue has changed significantly and you would be well advised to tax this car allowance by including it as part of the deductions in the trainee's salary.

Nevertheless, in order to assist your trainee, you may like to apply to the tax office dealing with your staff PAYE matters and see if they will grant you a dispensation. You should not attempt to ignore this allowance completely unless you have such an agreement from your tax office in writing, as this could well prove expensive at some later date. If a dispensation is not granted by the office, you should ask the trainee to either visit or write to the tax office, asking them for a claim form (P87), which will enable him to make a claim and he should then try and negotiate with the tax office so that the anticipated expenses of running his car for the practice are added to his code number. This will then mean that, although the car allowance is included with his taxable pay, the operation of a higher code number means that the actual tax charged will be reduced to a more reasonable level.

4

Partnerships in General Practice

▲ Question 25: Income tax in partnerships

I am a member of a partnership but am unable to understand how our income tax is calculated. Although there are five equal partners in the practice, we find our tax bills vary enormously between us and really cannot understand why this should be. Surely if we are equal partners we should pay the same amount of tax. Can you explain how this works?

There is in fact no reason whatsoever why your tax bills should be identical or even similar, even though you are equal partners in practice. Partnership tax assessments are in effect the total of the partners' individual tax bills and it would be unusual indeed if all your own personal circumstances were to be such that you all had identical tax liabilities.

Although you will indeed be taxed on an equal share of the practice profits, there will be many items to deduct from these before the actual tax liability is calculated. For instance, some of the partners may be claiming more motor expenses (*see* Questions 63–69) than the others, some of them may be paying salaries and pension premiums for their wives (*see* Questions 78–81), some of them may have large loans allowable for tax and many other items.

If necessary, ask your accountant to let you have a note of exactly how your own tax liability is calculated, tracing this from the figures shown in your partnership accounts. You have, however, no right to ask for an explanation of your partners' liabilities, unless of course they agree.

This system has changed completely following the introduction of self-assessment in 1996/97 (*see* Question 21).

▲ Question 26: Allocation of assessable partnership profits

I am a doctor in a partnership and my share is increasing to parity next year. My accountant has told me that this will bring a higher tax liability but I cannot understand why this is so. I thought that tax was assessed on profits earned in a previous year when my share of the profits was lower.

This is not in fact the case; the basic principle of the allocation of partnership profits for tax purposes, whether in a medical practice or any other business, is that the profits agreed for any accounting year, say to 30 June 1994, are assessable to tax in the following year of assessment (1995/96), but the profits are divided between the partners on the basis of their profit-sharing ratios within the year of assessment.

What this means in your own case is that, although the profits upon which your assessment is based were earned in a previous year, for tax purposes when they are assessed they must be divided between you in the profit-shares in the current tax year, in this case between 5 April 1995 and 5 April 1996.

If this seems a little unfair, please remember that you will be paying tax as a parity partner out of presumably higher earnings.

This system has now changed radically following the change to the current year basis of assessment (*see* Question 20).

▲ Question 27: Introduction of capital

I am a new partner in my practice and have been told that within the next year I shall be expected to contribute towards the capital of my partnership. The practice owns its own surgery and is a dispensing practice with a high stock of drugs. How much should I be expected to contribute? From where can I obtain the funds to do so and will I get tax relief for this?

The contribution you will be required to make to your partnership is likely to fall under two headings. You will make investments in the surgery premises and in the capital of the partnership, which is likely to include the current value of the fixed assets and the working capital.

The investment in the surgery should be made upon the basis of the equity in the building, that is, the current valuation less the balance on the outstanding mortgage, if any. Therefore if, say, the surgery was valued at £750 000 but there was a £550 000 mortgage on the building, this leaves an equity of £200 000. If you were buying a one-fifth share you would be expected to contribute capital of £40 000. From the date of purchase you would be entitled to receive an equivalent share of the notional or cost-rent allowance on the building but would at the same time make yourself liable to meet the cost of interest and capital repayments on the partnership mortgage.

The amount of the remaining capital of your practice depends very much on the facts of the case. As you are in a dispensing practice, this will normally mean that the working capital is very much higher than would otherwise be the case, and your contribution to the capital proportionally higher also. Remember, though, that you will be acquiring an interest in a higher level of income than would be the case were you a member of a non-dispensing practice.

The practice will also own normal fixtures and fittings, such as furniture, machinery, equipment and so on, which have a value, and it will also be required to hold funds as working capital to run the practice from day to day without incurring a bank overdraft. Again, if in your practice this capital in total was to be valued at say £50 000, you could reasonably be expected to buy one-fifth of this, that is, another £10 000.

You should have little difficulty in arranging a suitable source of finance. Many banks and the GP Finance Corporation offer facilities of this nature to doctors and are well-tuned to deal with requirements such as your own. The bank will charge you interest at whatever is the going rate but such interest will be allowable in full for tax purposes. You will obtain this tax relief on the basis of the actual year's interest incurred in a year of assessment, not on the preceding year basis (or from 1997/98, the current year basis) which is the case with other types of practice expenses. Make sure your bank gives you a certificate each year, which you should give to your accountant so that he can claim the interest through your annual tax return.

▲ Question 28: Relief for expenses on retirement

I shall shortly be retiring from practice. When I leave my partnership I have been told I will not receive tax relief for the expenses I incur in my last year of practice. I will be very much out of pocket on this. Is there anything I can do about it?

This was indeed a common problem up to the ending of the preceding year basis of assessment, which brought with it all manner of anomalies, particularly in the case of retiring GPs.

This particular anomaly has, however, now ended with the introduction of self-assessment, where GPs can be assured that they will receive tax relief on expenses incurred up to the date of their retirement. Retiring GPs also now have the assurance of knowing that their personal expenses will be allowed against their own share of the assessment and not those of their colleagues.

▲ Question 29: Progress to parity

We are taking a new partner into our practice. However, we have no idea what to pay him and how this could be calculated by steps to parity. Can you tell us how to proceed?

This very largely depends on the preferences of the partnership and the individual partner, taking into account local conditions and precedents set in the past.

The initial share of his profits will be based on the experience of the doctor concerned, his requirements, the nature and area of the practice covered, and would be subject to negotiation and agreement by the parties. A look through typical job announcements in the small 'ads' columns of medical journals will give you some idea of prevailing rates.

It is usual practice for new doctors to join on, say, a probationary period at a fixed share of the profits, converting to a percentage or fixed-share option after 6 months, and rising to parity in equal increments over 3 years. Some partnerships are prepared to offer parity over a shorter period.

Thus, where a practice with an annual profit of £300 000 offered a new partner an initial starting income of £30 000 per annum, this would represent a percentage option of 10% and it is normal in the first year or so to give the partner an opportunity of enhancing his income by stating that this will be at the level of £30 000 per annum or 10% of the profits, whichever is the greater. This of course should be clearly specified in the partnership deed.

If this is a five-partner practice, where parity would represent 20% of the profits, and it is common for an initial parity period to be 3 years, a new partner commencing at 10% for the first year could expect to reach parity with two annual increments, his percentage share of the profits rising to, say, 13.3% and 16.6% and to final parity at 20% after 3 years.

▲ Question 30: New partners: additional income

My practice is considering taking on a new partner. We are a practice of four doctors and our list sizes are now sufficient to justify a fifth partner. We are, however, concerned as to how this might affect our future incomes and I wonder if you could let me know exactly what additional allowances we shall receive for the new partner?

Provided that the engagement of a new partner has been properly approved by the Local Medical Committee and you have satisfied them that a legitimate vacancy exists, you will receive the basic practice allowance only for this additional partner. For the 1998/99 year this amounts to £7776 (i.e. from 1 April 1998).

You should, however, also take into consideration the fact that you may well have been paying out expensive locum fees to cater for the additional workload. The introduction of a new partner could mean that the practice can now dispense with this expenditure. The new partner may also be entitled to the postgraduate education allowance of £2445 although, depending on partnership policy, this can either be paid into practice funds or, if agreed, retained by the partner in whose name it is paid.

You should encourage the new partner to find extra sources of income, such as outside appointments, which will in turn enhance the total partnership income.

▲ Question 31: Treatment of seniority awards etc.

Do you think that practices where doctors earn seniority and similar awards should put these into the partnership pool of income for division, or should they retain them privately?

This really depends on the policy of the partnership; so long as the same principle applies to all of the partners there can really be no possibility of unfairness.

Most partnerships, however, maintain the principle, which should be clearly set out in the partnership deed, that awards of this nature are to be retained personally by the partners in whose names they are paid. In the case of seniority awards, this is a monetary recognition of long service in the profession, while the postgraduate education allowance (*see* also Question 30) to which the same principle applies, is a payment for having fulfilled certain requirements to attend a series of courses on clinical and other matters.

In many cases, the decision to pool or retain these items of income depends on the tradition of the practice and there can be no possibility of inequity between the partners, except insofar as a partner who had given long service to the profession could be contributing more to the partnership pool than would a younger partner.

One way in which some unfairness could occur is in the question of superannuation. By pooling this income, older partners are in effect foregoing some element of valuable superannuable income and this could lead to an eventual loss of pension benefit. This would be counteracted by electing for the partners to pay superannuation contributions on their own seniority awards, even though these are pooled for the purpose of allocating profits.

▲ Question 32: Medical earnings: out of hours work

After joining my partnership about a year ago I am now told that, according to our agreement, any fees I earn from medical work, even though I do this in my spare time, must be paid into the partnership. Can they make me do this?

I took an outside job working for a relief service one or two nights a week to supplement the family income and do not see why I should have to pay this into the practice.

If the partnership agreement, which presumably you have approved and signed, says that all medical income of the doctors should be paid into the practice funds, then you have no alternative but to do so. If you feel sufficiently strongly about it, you should approach your partners to see if they will agree to either the deed being amended or a suitable memorandum executed, which should be signed and witnessed by all the partners, in order to bring the required change into effect.

It is perhaps a pity that this question has arisen. You should have been made fully aware of any such provision in your partnership deed.

In fact, it is unlikely that you will be out of pocket by such a procedure. It is reasonable to assume that your partners also do work out of normal surgery hours and under the terms of the agreement they will also be required to pool this with partnership income. You will therefore effectively receive a share of those earnings.

If all else fails and you feel strongly about it as a matter of principle, then you may wish to consider leaving the partnership. This is, however, a somewhat extreme option which should only be considered as a last resort.

▲ Question 33: Accumulation of earnings in partnerships

I am moving to another part of the country and have provisionally arranged to join a new partnership, after resigning from my previous one.

After having a quick look at the proposed partnership deed of my new practice, I see that there is a proposal that all earnings of the partnership are paid into partnership funds for division. In my previous practice this did not happen; all the partners kept their own earnings apart from NHS income and I wonder if this is to be advocated.

This really depends on the policy and philosophy of separate partnerships. If you are joining a new practice then the concept of 'when in Rome do as the Romans do' applies – you should either accept the deed as presented to you, negotiate for amendment or, if you feel sufficiently strongly about it, look for another practice.

In principle, there is no objection whatsoever to the pooling of medical earnings by partners; indeed, it is strongly to be recommended. Not only does it give the partners the feeling of a single entity, all pulling in the same direction for the good of all, but it also brings the medical profession more into line with the practice in other similar professions. One rarely finds, for instance, accountants, lawyers or architects keeping part of their earnings to themselves – it is taken as read that they will all be paid into partnership funds.

Again, there is no real likelihood of any loss of income. What many doctors tend not to appreciate is that just as they are paying their own earnings into the partnership funds so also are their partners, so that the practice earnings, and hence their own share of those profits, will increase accordingly.

Experience tends to show that most efficient, well-organized partnerships with a proper tradition of financial discipline invariably pool all their earnings, apart from seniority, and in some cases night-visit fees, in the same manner as your new practice.

▲ Question 34: Partnership deeds

I have been in my practice now for several years and have been trying to persuade my partners to have a partnership deed drawn up. A few of them want one but the majority are either not prepared to pay the solicitors' fees or feel that as we are all reasonably friendly we will not have any dispute and it may not be necessary to go to the expense of having a deed. Do you think it is necessary to have a deed and, if so, what should be included in it?

Those partners who do not want a deed drawn up are being extremely obtuse and short-sighted. Rather sadly, rather less than half of the country's GP partnerships have a properly executed deed in force.

It cannot be too highly emphasized that all partnerships should have a properly drawn up deed, which if necessary should be amended by the drawing-up of a supplementary deed as and when partnership changes occur.

A properly drawn-up partnership deed is an essential protection for the partners against any disputes that might arise between them in the future. It is the document that governs the conduct of the partnership and relationships of the partners with each other. It should cover such items as: (a) partnership accounts; (b) definition of partnership income and expenditure; (c) division of profits; (d) arrangements to apply in the event of sickness; (e) retirement; and numerous other eventualities. A deed would cover not only those events that may occur but those that almost certainly will occur at some time, such as death, sickness and changes in profit-sharing ratios.

If the partnership does not have a deed, the practice will be governed by the terms of the Partnership Act 1890 and it is quite likely this will lead to disputes that would not have arisen had a properly drawn-up deed been in operation. The potential cost of legal proceedings or solicitors' charges on a dispute should alone be sufficient justification for ensuring that such a deed is in operation at all times.

Such a deed should ideally be drafted by a solicitor who is experienced in dealing with medical partnerships and should be examined before signature by an accountant who can display a similar speciality.

▲ Question 35: De-merger of partnership

I am a member of an eight-doctor practice, working from two separate locations, which is considering dividing into two. We do not get on and our philosophies of practice are quite different. We have therefore reluctantly come to the conclusion that it would be better if we were to practise separately, in two units of five and three doctors. At present we all divide profits equally and this division would continue under the new arrangement.

We are, however, worried that this might cause an extra tax liability if the partnership ceases and wonder how we can get round this.

Had your partnership de-merged before 6 April 1997, this may well have been a major issue and you could well have lost out in terms of tax. With the coming of the change to current year basis of assessment, however, the submission of a continuation election is no longer relevant. Each partner will now be assessed on his profits up to the date of such a dissolution and it is unlikely that a higher tax liability will arise.

▲ Question 36: Taxation and drawings

I am a parity partner in a five-doctor practice. Each month our practice manager works out our salaries and these are paid to us in variable amounts depending on how much money is available for distribution. At the same time she sets aside an amount for payment of future tax liabilities.

We have now been advised by our accountant that we have not drawn out our full entitlement and I have been advised I can take a further salary of £7248. I am extremely worried that this might cause me to pay further tax. I have asked both our practice manager and the accountant, who do not seem able to advise me fully. Can you help?

I am afraid that here you are becoming muddled between the nature of drawings and salaries. In medical finance, as in so many other walks of life, if one uses the correct terminology the problem frequently solves itself.

The amounts you draw out at the end of each month are not a salary but merely a drawing on account of your profits (*see* Question 8). You pay tax each year on your partnership share of the profits earned by your practice in the previous accounting year, less such practice expenses as you are able to negotiate (*see* Question 53).

In short, if you were to earn £40 000 in a year, this is the amount upon which you would be taxed, subject to normal adjustments, regardless of whether you drew out £35 000 or £45 000. Any amount you are now advised to withdraw from the practice, therefore, is presumably an adjustment to your current account balance (*see* Question 121) and you either have been or shortly will pay tax on the profits to which it relates. The mere withdrawal of this amount from your practice will not in itself, therefore, trigger an additional tax liability on your part.

5

Surgeries and Cost-rents

▲ Question 37: Surgery-related refunds

We own our own surgery and I think that, as well as the rent allowance, we can also get refunds for other types of expenditure that we have to pay out for the surgery. Can you tell me what these are?

Yes, there are several other refunds that you can obtain provided that claims are submitted properly.

Firstly, you can claim for all rates paid on the property; this includes business rates to the local authority and other items such as sewage, drainage, water and any similar types of rates that might be paid in your locality.

If your local authority is not prepared to take away trade refuse without payment, you can also claim the cost of this refuse collection.

On some occasions, where practices are situated in inner-city area or where there is no easy car-parking space, Health Authorities are empowered to refund in certain circumstances the cost of reserved parking spaces.

Please make sure that these claims are submitted both regularly and systematically. Failure to do so can very easily cost the partnership a great deal of money!

▲ Question 38: Notional rent assessment

We have just had a review of the notional rent on our practice premises and to our horror find that the District Valuer has proposed to reduce this from £30 000 per annum to £22 000 per annum. The partners rely on this as part of our practice income and we think it quite unacceptable that this has gone down. Is there anything we can do about it?

The District Valuer makes a revaluation of your notional rent every 3 years. In recent years it has become apparent that, largely due to the fall in commercial rents as a result of the property recession, some valuers have sought to seek a reduction in these assessments.

For most practices this is quite unacceptable and you must make entirely sure that you enter an appeal against this revaluation and do not accept it without objection.

You have the right of appeal to the Secretary of State and an inspector will be appointed to hear your case. If the matter reaches that stage you would be well advised to instruct a surveyor well versed in valuations of surgery premises, who will represent you and argue the case on your behalf.

As part of your argument it is suggested that you quote the provisions of SFA paragraph 51 schedule 4 2(a)(I). This clause sets out the manner in which such rent assessments are to be reviewed and provides for these to be based upon a 15-year lease providing for *upward only* reviews every 3 years.

▲ Question 39: Negative equity

I shall be retiring from my practice within the next 3 years. About 5 years ago the practice built a new surgery at a total cost of about £700 000, which was wholly financed by a bank loan. I have a fifth equal share in this building.

The property was valued only a few weeks ago at a sum of £400 000. We are still receiving cost-rent on the initial cost of £700 000. However, this appears to give a shortfall of £300 000.

I am appalled by the fact that I may be left with this debt hanging round my neck, possibly for several years after I retire. The partners have intimated to me that if there is no change in the valuation they will insist on me repaying the practice my share of the shortfall. Can they really do this?

You appear to have fallen into the classic 'negative equity' trap, which has been the lot of many practices, particularly in urban areas, during the fall in property values in recent years. There is no easy answer to this problem and the only possible crumb of comfort is that you are by no means the only GP finding himself in this position.

Some well-advised practices have for some years inserted a clause in their partnership deed which provides for exactly these circumstances. This would mean that a partner leaving the practice would find that the surgery was valued at the original cost price, for this purpose only, and would be fully covered by the mortgage. While he would not walk away with a profit, at least he would not be left with a liability hanging round his neck. If, as appears to be the case in your practice, no such provision exists, then one must fall back on other courses of action.

On the face of it, your partners have a perfect right to expect you to pay in your share of this negative equity. Property ownership has its risks, and these have been fully realized on this occasion. It may well be that this will take up a large proportion of your assets on retirement and obviously is a situation you would prefer to avoid if at all possible.

The only real alternative available to you would seem to be the retention of ownership of your share of the building, receiving from the practice your share of the rent allowance after retirement, but continuing to be responsible for your cost of servicing the mortgage. It may well be that you would be prepared to retain ownership of your share for some years, hoping that the valuation would increase as time went by. This will, of course, require the co-operation of your partners.

This is a situation where there is no real solution; merely the prospect of choosing the least objectionable of a number of highly unsatisfactory options.

▲ Question 40: Proceeds from surgery sale

I am proposing to retire from practice shortly and have an equal one-fifth share of the surgery, which was built within the last 10 years under the cost-rent scheme. An unofficial valuation gives the present value of the surgery as £500 000 but there is an existing mortgage on the property of £180 000.

How can I obtain my share of the surgery on retirement, and do I have to continue paying off this mortgage?

To some degree this depends on the wording of your partnership deed, but you will normally find that you would be entitled only to your share in the equity of the property at or within a specific period from the date of retirement. Using your figures this could be calculated as shown in Figure 3.

What would happen is that, on retirement, you would divest yourself both of the ownership of the surgery and any continuing commitment to the mortgage. This would either be paid by your continuing partners if they completed the purchase of your own share from you, or by direct sale to an incoming partner without involving the other partners in the transaction.

	£
Surgery valuation	500 000
Outstanding mortgage	180 000
Equity	320 000
Your 1/5th share	64 000

Figure 3: Example of sale of share of practice details on retirement.

▲ Question 41: Capital gains tax on surgery sale on retirement

I am retiring shortly and shall be selling my share in the surgery. I have owned the surgery for 20 years and shall be selling my share for a figure of about £200 000. The original cost was £80 000. I am aged 63 years and shall be retiring fully from practice.

Can you tell me if there will be any charge to me for Capital Gains Tax (CGT)?

Provided that you fulfil all the necessary criteria for the granting of Capital Gains Tax relief on retirement you will not have any CGT to pay on this sale.

These conditions are that you are over the age of 50 years and that you have owned the surgery for over 10 years. The overall gain over the period is £120 000 and, even without allowing for the various reliefs available, this is well within the exemption limit so that no CGT is payable. The current exemption limits are £250 000 in full and half the difference between £250 000 and £1 million. If the surgery had been owned by you for less than 10 years then the limit would be reduced proportionately.

As a result of the 1998 Budget, this relief will be gradually phased out and will no longer apply in the 2003/4 year. GPs owning surgeries may well consider selling their share before that date.

▲ Question 42: Cost-rent income

My practice is considering going in for a cost-rent scheme and has been looking at a project that is likely to cost us about £500 000 in total. Can you give me some idea as to how much income we will get from the surgery, and how often this will be paid to us?

The rule is that the cost-rent will be paid to you, dating from the time you commenced practice at the surgery, at whatever is the fixed or variable rate currently available, applied to the total cost of the project, where this falls within the cost-rent limits.

Upon your figure of £500 000 therefore, provided that it all falls within prescribed cost-rent limits, there could be applied the fixed rate at the time this reply is made, of 11%. This would therefore give the practice a cost-rent income of £55 000 per annum. Out of this you would have to meet the cost of servicing any loans that you raise to finance the development.

There is an alternative facility available at a variable rate, currently 6.25% (for 1997/98), which rises and falls in accordance with prevailing rates, being adjusted on 1 April each year. There will be an opportunity to elect for the alternative notional rent basis at triennial intervals after taking up occupation in the new surgery. This may well be to your advantage at, say, 6 or almost certainly 9 years after the new surgery is brought into operation.

Any cost-rent income would be paid to you quarterly, or if you prefer, at monthly intervals. There may be an initial delay in having the final cost-rent allowance agreed by the Health Authority but, until then, it would be normal for this to be paid on a provisional basis, after taking up occupation of the building.

▲ Question 43: Tax treatment of rent allowances

I am an owner of the surgery premises in which my practice operates. We are a practice of six doctors, two of whom are part-time with the other four partners owning the surgery premises. We receive a notional rent allowance of £60 000 per annum.

Our accountant tells us that this is rental income and we must show it in our income tax returns, rather than being dealt with through the partnership accounts. Is this correct?

No, it is not correct. This income is paid to you by virtue of your terms of engagement with the National Health Service and is part of your earned income from the practice. As such, it should be treated as part of partnership income for assessment under Schedule D, allocated of course only to those partners owning the premises (*see* Question 44). It would be quite incorrect for it to be shown on your income tax return, where it might be taxed as investment income, with possible unfortunate results, including the possible eventual loss of your Capital Gains Tax retirement relief (*see* Question 41).

There is a common misunderstanding over the tax treatment of this income. The position is as outlined above but, unfortunately, the use of the term 'rent' tends to be misunderstood. This is more in the nature of an acknowledgement of the use of the doctor's privately owned premises in the National Health Service and is certainly not a rent within the strict definition of the term. A rent is a payment that normally passes from a tenant to a landlord and clearly this is not the case here, there being no conventional 'landlord/tenant' situation.

Your accountant should be aware of this principle, which is potentially extremely important to you.

▲ Question 44: Allocation of rent allowances: partnerships

I am one of four partners owning shares in our surgery. There are another three partners (one full-time partner and two part-time partners) who do not own any part of the surgery.

Our accountant tells us that we have got to share the rent allowance between us in the proportion in which we share practice profits. Is this correct? It does not seem right to me that partners who do not own the surgery should get a share of the rent allowance.

You are quite right; the notional (or cost) rent allowance on a surgery is considered to be a return on capital invested by the partners in return for their shares of ownership. Under no circumstances should it be shared between the partners in any other ratios.

This is normally performed by many accountants by treating the net proceeds from the surgery ownership as a prior share of profits (which might also include rents from third parties) and dividing this between the partners in the shares in which they own the surgery.

If you have a loan on the property, the capital repayments and interest cost of this should also be shared between the partners in ownership ratios and not in the ratios in which you share practice profits.

▲ Question 45: Rent and rates: health centres

I am in a partnership of three doctors practising in a health centre. We do not pay any amounts in respect of rent, rates and water charges for our accommodation in the health centre and I understand that these are reimbursed directly by the Health Authority (HA). I have been told that we should show these in our accounts but I cannot see how this should be done and our accountant does not understand why we should show in the accounts any figures that have not actually passed through our books.

Can you tell me why we should show these amounts and how the figures can be obtained?

The Review Body that reports each year on doctors' pay and allowances derives the figures, from which the annual calculations are made, from a sampling process taken from tax returns submitted by GPs each year to HM Inspector of Taxes.

As part of this sampling process, an average is taken of the amount of expenses charged by GPs through their practice accounts each year, and it is this average that is used in determining the indirectly reimbursable element in your pay each year.

It follows, therefore, that it is in the interests of the profession as a whole for doctors to maximize the amount of expenditure going through their accounts in order to assist this sampling process and ultimately to enhance the national average of expenditure.

The figure should be obtained from your HA. Some HAs are more co-operative and understanding in supplying these figures than others. You should insist on them being supplied to you. If all else fails, estimates may be included on both sides of the accounts, although this should only be done as a last resort.

Your accountant should understand the principle behind this and why it is necessary therefore to show, on both sides of your accounts, firstly the actual reimbursement of the rent and rates and, secondly the notional amount paid, even though these do not actually pass through your own books of account. This is in accordance with BMA/GMSC policy. Please see also the note following paragraph 53.4 in the Statement of Fees and Allowances (Red Book).

Some HAs have in recent years introduced a system whereby annual demands for rates and water rates are sent directly to them, and a payment is then made to the local authority. This relieves the practice from the cash flow problems of making a payment and receiving it back a few weeks later. Do be careful, however, that each year you receive from the HA a statement saying how much they have paid on your behalf. This must be brought into your accounts on both sides (*see* Question 122) so as to give a true reflection of your income and expenditure.

You would be well advised to consider using the services of an accountant who understands how GP finance works (*see* Question 106).

▲ Question 46: Rent payable by non-surgery-owning partners

We are a seven-doctor practice, in which the five senior partners all own the surgery premises in equal shares. We have two other partners, one a young doctor working his way to parity and a part-time doctor, both of whom are profit-sharing partners but who have not bought into the surgery premises.

It has been suggested that, in order to protect the partners against any fall in the cost-rent allowance, those non-property-owning partners should pay a rent for the share of accommodation they use. Can we do this?

You can, of course, do this if all the parties agree. Whether it is in your interests to do so is rather another matter.

It is a principle of medical finance that where GPs pay rent they can claim a refund of the cost. Presumably, therefore, if those two partners were to pay any rent they could claim a refund from the HA. The HA may well decline to pay a refund, which would leave those two doctors considerably out of pocket.

As you are getting the cost-rent allowance, the HA is entitled to deduct from this any rent you receive from outside sources and presumably those two doctors would for that purpose be so defined.

The fact is that the surgery-owning partners receive recompense in the form of the cost-rent allowance for the use of the surgery, which is not shared by the non-owning partners (*see* Question 44). This effectively represents their return on their investment in the premises.

GPs who find themselves in your position should be strongly discouraged from seeking to charge rent in circumstances such as you have outlined and it is not normally done.

▲ Question 47: Abatement of direct refunds

Much of our income is from private patients and non-NHS sources. Our Health Authority (HA) is now trying to reduce our refunds for rent, rates and ancillary staff for this reason. Is this right and is there anything we can do about it?

Your HA may be quite right in abating your direct refunds for rent, rates and staff for this reason, but there may well be something you can do about it. This abatement will normally apply only if your income from non-NHS sources is more than 10% of your gross income.

The same paragraph in the Statement of Fees and Allowances (Red Book) that provides for these abatements also states that the required proportion goes up to 15% if there are any other surgeries in use apart from those funded under the NHS scheme. There may be circumstances in which you can make use of this provision. For instance, your HA may be prepared to accept the doctors' private houses as surgeries under this heading, provided that fees are earned from there.

In addition, the abatement only applies to fees actually earned from NHS-financed premises or with NHS staff. If you can clearly show that much of the work is done and fees earned away from your surgery and without using your own staff, you can quite properly claim that this is the case and your HA should be prepared to accept this. Some practices which find themselves in this position arrange their affairs so that fees from, for example, insurance medicals and private patients are effectively earned from the partners' private houses, which means that you can complete the required certificate for the HA each year.

Detailed conditions for abatement of certain direct refunds are set out in paragraph 51.15 of the Statement of Fees and Allowances (Red Book).

▲ Question 48: Income on surgery ownership after retirement

I shall shortly be retiring from practice. For most of my career I have been a joint owner in the surgery building and expect to receive a share of this on retirement. I have agreed with my partners that I will delay receipt of the money from this sale until at the most 1 year after the date of my retirement. I understand this is beneficial for tax reasons.

However, I think I am entitled to an income from the surgery after I retire and I wonder how this will work. Do I get a share of the notional rent?

First, let us deal with the tax question. You are correct in saying that if you delay the sale of your share of the surgery for a period of no more than 1 year then you will not lose the Capital Gains Tax retirement relief which one would normally expect to be available to you (*see* Question 41).

For this to be of value, you should first of all check to see that you will have a capital gain to charge, which has been of some doubt in recent years.

As regards the payment of income to you deriving from your continued ownership of a share of the surgery, you are quite right and quite clearly some such payment should in all equity be made to you until you receive the money. Ideally this should be set down in your partnership deed, which should say exactly how the partnership proposes to compensate you in such circumstances.

Some practices continue to pay the share of the rent allowance to the retired GP but this may not be satisfactory, particularly if the partnership has a continuing mortgage on the surgery and the retired partner will also be expected to pay his share of this. This also tends to be extremely untidy and complex for tax reasons as the doctor is no longer a partner and cannot share in the partnership tax assessment for that year.

What many practices do is to agree to pay the retired partner at an agreed rate of interest, which may well be 2% over the minimum lending rate for the time being. This ranks as taxable income in the hands of the retired doctor but is a tax deductible expense against the practice; and, more specifically, the partners who own the surgery.

▲ Question 49: Cost-rent finance

We are thinking of building a new surgery and will need to borrow a large amount of money. To whom should we go to obtain this?

There are many sources of finance available to GPs for building surgery premises; the problem is not so much to find the money but which is the best source available.

Several of the major banks now offer funds to GPs for buying surgeries and are quite likely to be able to help. You would be well advised to 'shop around' with a view to obtaining the best deal available. The GP Finance Corporation also offers realistic terms for finance of this nature.

National Westminster, TSB and Royal Bank of Scotland are banks which have been prominent in this field in recent years and tend to understand the requirements of GPs embarking on schemes of this nature.

You may wish to avoid schemes where the repayment of funds is linked to a life assurance endowment policy or some private pension scheme. This is likely to make the scheme far more expensive and, while it may be beneficial in the long term, many schemes tend to be expensive in their early years and you will want to cut down your early expenses as much as you can. Try also to avoid borrowing from different sources as this could lead to higher interest charges.

You can obtain bridging finance during the development period and many practices defer making a final decision on the ultimate source of long-term borrowing until the project is almost complete. Interest on this bridging finance will be 'rolled-up' and is aggregable with the total cost of the project upon which the final cost-rent will be calculated.

Without a doubt, specialist and knowledgeable advice is essential. It is difficult to offer current advice as interest rates change regularly and up-to-date advice can only be given with a knowledge of prevailing conditions in the market. You should ensure that your adviser **is** independent and that there is no conflict of interest.

▲ Question 50: Surgery: sole ownership

I am the sole owner of our surgery premises, which are occupied by our practice of six partners. I shall shortly be retiring and selling the property. Will I be able to claim any retirement relief?

I think what you are talking about is the Capital Gains Tax (CGT) retirement relief which, if you are over 50 years of age, is likely to apply to you (*see* Question 41).

However, in similar circumstances GPs have had their entitlement to CGT retirement relief scaled down on the grounds that they have only been in occupation of part (in your case, one-sixth) of the building. For this reason, you should not assume that your claim for this relief is no more than a formality. You (or more likely your accountant) may well be involved in some difficult negotiations before the relief is granted, if at all.

This calls into question the policy of only one practice partner owning the surgery premises. Owing to the problems of continuity and succession, it is not usually considered good practice for this to be the case and most partnerships would be well advised to spread the ownership of the building among the partners, so far as this is practical.

6

Value Added Tax

▲ Question 51: VAT on new surgeries

My practice is proposing, in the near future, to build a new surgery under the cost-rent scheme. A plot of land has been identified, a price agreed and plans have been prepared.

Can you advise us of the present position as regards VAT on this development? We understand that VAT will be charged by the architect and the builder. Can we get this back?

For some years there was a scheme, known as the 'self-supply scheme' under which GPs building surgeries were deemed to be property developers and were required to register for VAT if the total cost of the project exceeded a certain figure.

This scheme has, however, now ceased and you will not be required to register for VAT in connection with this project.

A major feature of the 'self-supply scheme' was that practices were ultimately required to pay VAT on the total cost of the land. This will no longer be necessary.

Practices developing surgeries will still be required to bear the cost of VAT on any payments to architects, builders and other professionals. This will not be refunded directly to them, as GPs are not registered traders and will therefore be unable to cover such a cost in their normal quarterly returns.

You should, however, ensure that your cost-rent reimbursement is calculated at the full scale (Rate A), which effectively includes VAT. While the VAT will not be refunded directly to you, it will be reflected in a higher rate of cost-rent reimbursement you will receive than would otherwise be the case.

▲ Question 52: VAT: partial exemption scheme

I am a GP in practice and pay quite a lot of money out in VAT – on telephone bills, professional fees, repairs and now on lighting and heating costs. I understood there was a scheme where I could register for VAT and get this back. How do I go about this?

You are referring to the partial exemption ('toothbrush') scheme, which was in existence for certain professions which would otherwise be unable to register for VAT. The scheme commenced in 1992, but was effectively abolished by the Budget in November 1994. This scheme ceased from 1 December 1994 and you will therefore now be unable to register for VAT.

The GPs' position now reverts to that which applied before the introduction of the partial exemption scheme in that they are not required to charge VAT by adding this to patients' fees. By the same token, neither can they recover input tax (i.e. VAT paid) in any way.

This is an additional cost to your practice and can be claimed for income tax purposes by including all such expenditure in your accounts under the appropriate heading.

In the case of GPs only, it will be indirectly refunded to them through the indirect expenses element included in their annual remuneration award.

In certain circumstances, dispensing practices can register for VAT but the regulations are complex and those practices would be well advised to seek specialist help.

7
Practice Expenses

▲ Question 53: Practice expenses in partnerships

I shall shortly be taking up a partnership. Some of the expenses of the partnership will be paid from partnership funds and some will have to be paid by me. How will I obtain tax relief for these?

Those expenses that are paid out of partnership funds and agreed by the terms of the partnership deed to be expenses of the practice will be shown in the partnership accounts and allowed against the partnership profits for tax purposes, being in effect divided in agreed ratios from time to time. Unless there are any extremely unusual items, these would usually be allowed for tax purposes without undue enquiry.

Such expenses as you might pay yourself in connection with your practice will be allowed either wholly or partially for tax purposes by submission of your own annual claim for personal practice expenses, probably by your own accountants (*see* Question 104). This is likely to include such items as: (a) your car expenses; (b) possibly use of your house in the practice; (c) a spouse's salary and pension contributions; (d) a proportion of your private telephone bills; and (e) medical subscriptions and so on. This claim should be made up to the same date as your partnership's annual accounting year-end.

Policy between partnerships can vary widely as to which expenses are payable by the partnership and which by the individual partners. This should be clearly set out and defined in your partnership deed. However, provided that the claims are submitted to HM Inspector of Taxes in a reasonable form by a knowledgeable accountant, you should have little difficulty in obtaining tax relief on such part of this expenditure as the Inspector can agree has been spent wholly and exclusively in connection with your practice.

▲ Question 54: 'Duality of purpose'

I have been claiming practice expenses for several years without query by the Inspector of Taxes. He has now raised with my accountant the fact that some of the amounts I claim represent figures that should have been reduced after deduction for private use. I am thinking here specifically of house expenses, telephone bills and bank charges.

I understand that there is some Inland Revenue principle regarding such items. Does it mean that I cannot claim for these at all?

Firstly, there is an Inland Revenue principle concerned, known as the doctrine of 'duality of purpose'. By this means the Inland Revenue seeks to show that, where expenditure is incurred predominantly for a private purpose and only a small amount is applicable to business use, then the whole of the expenditure will be disallowed.

In the case of most doctors, this can be overcome by showing that the expenditure was incurred primarily for a practice purpose but that there also exists some private element that it is reasonable to deduct. In all cases you quote, it is reasonable to assume that the main purpose of the expenditure was business but that there is some element of private use.

The most difficult question to overcome is probably the one of house expenses (*see* Question 56).

Negotiations of this type depend very much upon the skill of the accountant dealing with the Inspector of Taxes. Provided that he is sufficiently experienced and understands the facts of the case and the principles involved, you may well find that the Inspector is more interested in trying to reduce the proportion of the claim somewhat than in disallowing the expenditure in its entirety.

▲ Question 55: Child minding

I am a female doctor in practice and have young children. The only way I can carry on my practice is to use the services of a child minder. Sometimes I take my children to her to look after, sometimes I engage another person to come and stay in the house during the year. Otherwise, I would be unable to work. Can I obtain relief on this expenditure for tax purposes?

No, unfortunately you cannot. In the eyes of the Inland Revenue, this is not expenditure in connection with your practice but to enable you to carry on the practice in the first place, which is construed as rather a different matter. The subject has been well tested and under no circumstances will this relief be granted by HM Inspector of Taxes.

A minor relaxation in the rules applies only to employees who have child-minding facilities provided by their employers. A concession has been agreed where female barristers can, in certain circumstances, claim relief for child-minding expenses. It is by no means clear whether this will be extended to GPs but any claim is unlikely to succeed, depending largely on the attitude of the local tax office.

▲ Question 56: Claims for use of house

I am a GP in practice and live quite near the surgery. I see patients fairly regularly at my home and believe there is some scheme by which I can obtain tax relief on the cost of running the house. Can you advise me how to go about this?

If there is a genuine element of practice use of your house, a claim for part of the running costs will be perfectly justified.

It is normal for these claims to be calculated by adding the total running costs of the house, including such items as Council Tax, lighting and heating, repairs and renewals, cleaning, insurance and similar items. No capital items such as the cost of extending or improving the property should be included.

When this total is obtained, a fraction is applied, which is likely to be about one-fifth to one-tenth, depending on the nature of the accommodation available and the proportion this bears to the total size of the house. For instance, if a doctor uses two rooms in a fairly small house he will have a much higher proportion of claim than one who uses two rooms of a very large house. The actual monetary amount of the claim may, of course, not be much different.

It is also recommended that, in order to substantiate a claim, several considerations be borne in mind.

1 The house should be within, or reasonably adjacent to, the practice area.
2 There should be a regular element of patient use.
3 Accommodation should be available, but not necessarily exclusively, for the use of patients when they call.
4 A plate should be exhibited outside the property.
5 There should be an appropriate entry in the local telephone directory.
6 The practice car(s) should be garaged there.

Although it is not necessary for all these conditions to apply when making a claim, they could be of considerable help.

Most GPs in this position can justify use of their house to the Inspector of Taxes by pointing out that they are required, under the terms of their contract of engagement with the NHS, to provide 24-hour cover for patients. If the surgery is only open during normal surgery hours it follows that the consulting and advising of patients can only be continued from the house of the partner on duty. It is likely also that the partners will have in force a partnership deed, which hopefully will include some provision that they are to occupy a suitable property that can be used for practice purposes if necessary.

It is not recommended that a claim of this nature is submitted unless the GP can display a clear pattern of practice use of the house. If not, and the house is used for administration, study, report-writing and the like, it will almost certainly be beneficial to submit a claim for a lump-sum study allowance.

In certain other situations, you may be able to justify an additional claim if you can clearly show that some areas of the house are used 'wholly and exclusively' for patient use, without any domestic use whatsoever. In such situations, there is little need for concern at possible Capital Gains Tax (CGT); the reliefs available make it extremely unlikely that any CGT will be payable. In such a situation it may also be possible to claim an additional proportion of mortgage interest relief (*see* Question 61).

▲ Question 57: Conference expenses

Can I claim tax relief for attending, with my wife, a BMA conference that is held overseas?

You can claim any expenses you wish; whether they are ultimately allowed by the HM Inspector of Taxes is a very different matter. In the case of overseas conferences, you should by no means assume that tax relief will automatically be given. The situation is at best uncertain and is confused by the fact that different Inspectors of

Taxes may well treat this expenditure in different ways. What one Inspector may be prepared to allow, another will disallow.

If, however, you are able to persuade the Inspector that the prime purpose of your journey was for clinical reasons to assist you in your practice, it will be of great benefit in pursuing the claim. If the Inspector believes that the main reason for your visit was a holiday and that the conference was merely incidental, he will almost certainly seek to disallow it. It would be as well to keep a note of the conference programme for production if required.

If your wife accompanies you on the journey, you will be unable to claim expenses for her unless you can show quite clearly that her presence was necessary for your practice. This would only be relevant if she was actually employed by the practice and was fulfilling a useful function in attending.

Doctors attending conferences of this nature are strongly advised to make claims for expenditure incurred by themselves, so far as this was not refunded to them. They should, however, accept that if the Inspector seeks to disallow it they have little alternative but to accept that decision.

▲ Question 58: Examination fees

I have recently taken the examination for the Royal College of Surgeons for which I was obliged to pay an examination fee. Can I claim this fee against tax? I am a GP in practice.

No. Examination fees are excluded from allowable expenses for tax purposes. In the eyes of the Inland Revenue, they are not, strictly speaking, expenses of running your practice but are incurred in obtaining a professional qualification, which in their eyes is an entirely different matter.

▲ Question 59: Video recorders

I am a partner in a training practice and as the nominated trainer I am considering buying a video recorder and camera for use by my trainees. Would this be allowable for tax purposes?

Relief will be granted on the purchase of this equipment if it can clearly be shown to the Inland Revenue that it is for practice use and for no other purpose.

If such a piece of equipment is purchased from partnership funds and is housed in the surgery premises, where it can quite clearly be used for practice purposes only, again you are likely to receive full income tax relief at current rates of capital allowance, 25% on the cost or written-down value.

However, if the video recorder is purchased by one of the partners and included in his own expenses claim, the equipment presumably being kept in his own house, it is less likely that full relief will be available. The Inspector would, at best, insist on a restriction for private use as he will assume, quite reasonably, that it is being used for domestic purposes also. In this latter connection, *see* Question 54.

▲ Question 60: Clothing

I am a GP in practice and purchase several suits a year for work. Can I claim the cost of these or cleaning them as a tax-deductible expense?

This answer to this is no. This has been tested in the courts and it is now virtually impossible to claim relief for clothing of this nature, which can also be used for normal social purposes, against your practice profits.

In this context, the Inland Revenue will almost certainly quote the doctrine of duality of purpose (*see* Question 54) and there seems to be little point in pursuing claims of this nature, unless it is necessitated by attendance (by the GP) at an accident or an incident within the practice.

You will be able to obtain tax relief in full if you purchase any protective clothing, such as a white coat, overalls and so on, which are intended for practice use only. Similarly, it may be possible for you to obtain some element of relief for the cost of cleaning your clothes although this is likely to be of a modest nature only.

▲ Question 61: Extra mortgage interest relief

I have a loan on my house of £50 000 and I also practise from home in addition to using our own surgery. Can I claim any additional tax relief on this interest?

You are eligible for tax relief on the interest on loans on your private house up to a statutory maximum of £30 000 capital, but from 6 April 1998 the tax relief is restricted to 10% only.

Whether you can claim any more than this depends on your Inspector of Taxes and the manner in which such claims are put to him. If you can clearly and genuinely show that part of your house is used wholly and exclusively for seeing patients and dealing with practice matters then you can claim tax relief on a proportionate amount of the loan interest, the proportion being the percentage of the house that is used solely for business purposes.

If, for instance, you are able to meet this latter criterion and the Inspector accepts a claim of 20% on your house expenses (*see* Question 56) you may also claim tax relief on 20% of your mortgage interest giving an additional £10 000 (i.e. 20% of £50 000) in addition to your statutory £30 000 maximum, making £40 000 in all. The tax relief on the interest on the further £10 000 would be eligible for relief at the top rate of tax.

You should claim such extra interest through your practice expenses claim and the tax relief would therefore be allowed as any other practice expense on the current year basis, effectively at your top rate of tax, which may well be 40%. Contrast this with the relief of only 10% you are receiving in respect of your basic mortgage interest relief.

▲ Question 62: Sickness insurance premiums

Each month I pay out premiums to cover the possible cost of paying locums if I am to be away from work through accident or illness. I am told that I cannot get tax relief for these premiums, which seems most unfair.

You have been mis-advised on this point. The attitude of the Inland Revenue towards premiums of this nature changed following a press release in April 1996.

The position now is that if you pay premiums on genuine locum insurance policies, i.e. those which provide only for a refund of locum costs in the event of your absence through sickness, then those premiums will be fully allowable for tax purposes. However, where such premiums are claimed, then if there is at some time a benefit paid under the policy, that benefit will fall into charge to tax. If you incur any actual locum costs during a period of sickness, then those locum costs will be allowable in full without question.

You may have been confused here by the question of permanent health insurance (or sickness) policies, which provide for a lump sum to be paid in the event of absence through sickness, regardless of the reason for which it is used. These policies continue to be ineffective for tax purposes.

8

Cars and Travelling

▲ Question 63: Cars: time to purchase

I am a GP in practice and have to consider buying a new car. My present car is 5 years old and expensive in repairs and maintenance. Should I change my car to obtain some tax relief?

I receive relief for car expenses against my practice income and believe there is one time that is more beneficial than others for changing my car. Could you please advise me of this?

You would be ill-advised to change your car purely for tax reasons as you would be out of pocket on the deal. However, in your case you could justify changing your car for sound economic reasons.

You should aim to change your car as soon as possible before your annual accounting year-end – not to be confused with the tax year-end of 5 April. If your practice or partnership therefore makes its accounts up to, say, 30 June each year, you should try and change your car as soon as possible before that date, rather than say on 2 or 3 July. The reason for this is that you will receive the capital allowances a year earlier than would otherwise have been the case.

If, for instance, you bought the new car on 28 June 1998 you would receive tax relief in the 1998/99 tax year; if you were to put back the purchase even for a few days to early July you would not be able to claim the tax relief until the 1999/2000 year.

▲ Question 64: Financing car purchase

I am considering buying a new car. Depending on the cost I am not sure whether I should pay for it out of my own funds or whether to borrow the money.

In general, what is the best way of purchasing a new car?

Firstly, you would be well advised to look around car showrooms to see if any are offering free loans for car purchase. Main agents may also be offering loans at low rates of interest.

Secondly, if you have sufficient free capital available, for instance in a bank or building society, it would be to your benefit to buy the car out of this money. You would thus avoid expensive interest charges, which would be higher than any interest you might receive on investment of these funds.

Failing this, the next best available source of finance is likely to be your bank. The major banks will usually offer business development loans for purchase of business assets, as would be the case here. These offer competitive fixed rates of interest, so long as the car is mainly for practice use. Full tax relief will be available on the loan interest, subject to any agreed disallowance for private use.

There are several sources available but it would not be advisable to use a hire purchase scheme except as a last resort if funds cannot be obtained elsewhere, due to the high rates of interest that would be charged.

▲ Question 65: Leasing cars

I am thinking of replacing my car and do not have the finance available to put down a lump sum. I am attracted to the prospect of leasing a car but I have heard it is not sound practice for GPs to do this. Can you tell me why?

The main reason why GPs are discouraged from leasing cars is that, because they are not registered for VAT (*see* Question 52), they are unable to recover the VAT included with each leasing premium. Under a leasing contract, VAT is charged on the whole payment including the interest element, whereas no VAT is chargeable on bank interest.

However, there are many different leasing schemes on the market and each one should be judged on its merits. Shop around, and if in any doubt, seek professional advice.

▲ Question 66: Cars: capital allowances

I joined a practice recently and am using the car I bought about 3 years ago for £8500. I have not previously made any claim for use of this car.

I understand that I can claim a 25% annual allowance for the use of the car but can this be claimed on the original purchase price or do I have to have the car valued when I join the practice?

The car should be valued at the open market value, according to the best evidence available at the time you joined the practice, and the 25% annual writing-down allowance is claimed on that figure. If, therefore, the value is seen to be £5000 at that date, the first year's allowance would be £1250.

▲ Question 67: Expensive cars

I am considering buying a new car but the one I want will cost £18 000. I also have another practice car which cost £8000 3–4 years ago. I understand there is a ceiling above which I cannot claim capital allowances for tax purposes. Can you explain how this works? What happens if I sell the car?

There is a ceiling of £12 000 for each car purchased since 11 March 1992. It does not apply to groups of cars, so the fact that you already have a car in use need not necessarily affect the allowance on the new car you are proposing to buy.

The ceiling works in that the normal 25% is restricted so that it cannot exceed £3000 p.a. This will be taken off in the first year and the system of allowances and written-down values will work as shown in Figure 4.

▲ Question 68: Trainee car allowance

I am a GP registrar and on joining my practice I was told by my employer that he had to deduct tax from my car allowance. Is this right and do the same deductions apply to National Insurance and superannuation?

The trainee car allowance is not subject to NHS superannuation contributions. It is likely, however, to be charged to Class 1 National Insurance, but only on any profit element, that is, the amount by which the car allowance exceeds any agreed car expenses.

With regard to income tax, there are several options open to the trainee and his trainer, with regard to the taxation of this allowance.

1 The trainer can apply to the tax office dealing with his PAYE affairs for a dispensation to be granted, which will lead to no tax being deducted from the car allowance.

	£	Actual allowed (say 80%) £
Cost	18 000	
First year:		
Annual allowance: 25%	3 000*	2400
	15 000	
Second year:		
Annual allowance: 25%	3 000*	2400
	12 000	
Third year:		
Annual allowance: 25%	3 000*	2400
	9 000	
Fourth year:		
Annual allowance: 25%	2 250	1800
	6 750	
Fifth year:		
Annual allowance: 25%	1 688	1350
	5 062	
Sale proceeds	4 000	
Balancing allowance	1 062	850

Figure 4: Example of written-down values and tax allowances for purchase of car.

*In respect of the first 3 years the same amount is written-off, that is £3000, as for the first 2 of those years a 25% reduction would have brought a higher figure. Provided a car is kept for a sufficiently long period, there is not necessarily any long-term loss to the GP owning a car in such circumstances. On the sale of the car, full relief is given on the net cost of the car, that is the cost less sale proceeds, by means of a balancing allowance, or a balancing charge if too much tax relief has been given.

2 The trainee himself can apply to the local tax office at the start of his trainee period and ask that a figure be included in his Notice of Coding, which will then give him a higher tax threshold. If the new code is applied it will have the same result as if the allowance had not been taxed at all. It will almost certainly be necessary

for him to submit a full and documented claim at the end of the period.
3 The trainee can keep a full list of all expenses, including car running expenses incurred during his trainee period, and submit a claim to HM Inspector of Taxes after the end of the year so that he will be entitled to a tax rebate. Claims should be submitted on form P87, which is available from tax offices.

It must be emphasized that the trainer is within his rights, unless he has obtained a dispensation as set out in 1 above, in making these PAYE deductions on the car allowance. If he does not do so, and the Inland Revenue discovers the error, possibly some years afterwards, he can be held personally liable for the amount of tax that should have been deducted. *See* Question 24.

▲ Question 69: Mileage logs

I have been told by my accountant that I should keep some form of record of miles I travel in my car to claim some tax relief. Do I really have to do this and how does it work?

If you are to avoid Inland Revenue enquiries into your car-expenses claim and any possible adverse consequences, you would be well advised to produce some form of mileage log for a period of, say, 2 typical months, in order to establish an agreed restriction for private use.

It is, however, unnecessary to keep a permanent mileage log and hopefully it would not prove too inconvenient to maintain a log for just a few months.

Figure 5 is an illustration of how such a mileage log might look. Remember that routine journeys between home and the surgery represent private mileage unless patients are visited en route.

Cars and travelling • 73

This advice has become even more relevant with the introduction of self-assessment and the possibility of GPs being selected for 'random audits' by the Inland Revenue.

Mileage logs: June/July 1998						
		ROVER Miles			MONDEO Miles	
	Total	Practice	Private	Total	Practice	Private
Week ended:						
June 5	475	420	55	63	20	43
12	125	50	75	385	195	190
19	578	300	278	75	15	60
26	487	400	87	88	8	80
July 3	569	525	44	56	16	40
10	87	20	67	468	170	298
17	625	557	68	42	24	18
24	480	404	76	50	38	12
31	360	350	10	68	34	34
Total (2 months)	3786	3026	760	1295	520	775
Percentages		79.9	20.1		40.2	59.8

Figure 5: Example of mileage log for two cars for 2 months.

9

Capital Taxes

▲ Question 70: Capital Gains Tax on sale of shares

I have some shares that I am thinking of selling. I have held them for several years and wonder exactly how the gain would be calculated and what reliefs are available.

The gain would be calculated by taking the proceeds of sale and deducting from this the actual price at which you bought the shares, allowing for any commission and charges. If there is a gain you could reduce this further by applying the indexation relief, which is a fixed percentage depending on the date you sold the shares and the length of time you held them. The calculation is based on percentages, which are published monthly. This relief is intended to cover the effect of inflation on share prices and asset values over the period held.

If you bought the shares before 1982, the cost price will be adjusted to the value at 6 April 1982, so that any gains accruing before that date will fall out of charge to tax. This system is known as re-basing. In addition, there is an annual exemption limit, which changes from year to year. For 1998/99, this limit is £6800 each, for both husband and wife. *See* Question 71.

If you have sold the shares at a loss, you can offset against any other gains made on sales of assets during the same tax year or carry the loss forward to future years where it can be set against gains made at the time.

▲ Question 71: Capital Gains Tax: annual exemption

I may be selling some assets, including a house, during the coming year. Do I get any Capital Gains Tax (CGT) relief for this?

Unless the house is your main private residence or an asset of your trade or profession, there is no actual relief available. Once you have worked out the gain, applying any re-basing and indexation reliefs (*see* Question 70), you will have to pay CGT at your top rate of tax on this, over and above the annual exemption, which is the first £6800 of gains in the 1998/99 tax year (£13 600 for a married couple). Therefore, if your chargeable gain (after re-basing and indexation relief) was, say, £9000, you would have tax to pay on the amount by which this exceeded £6800, in other words £2200. At say 40%, the cost in terms of actual tax payable would be £880, assuming there were no other gains during the same tax year.

If the property was your private dwelling (including any garden up to half a hectare) any gain on this would be exempt.

▲ Question 72: Inheritance Tax

I am a married male doctor aged 59 years and wish to retire shortly. I am worried that if I die within the next few years my estate will be chargeable to a great deal of Inheritance Tax. On retirement, after selling my share of the surgery, my lump-sum retiring allowance and certain insurance policies, which will fall in, together with the value of my own house and some investments, my total estate will be worth about £800 000. Should I do anything to try and minimize the charge to Inheritance Tax?

There are legal ways which you can use to avoid Inheritance Tax (IHT) in the event of your untimely death. For the year 1998/99, the threshold over which IHT will be levied is £223 000. Above that limit, tax will be charged at 40%.

There are many ways in which you might try to alleviate such a charge. Firstly, you would be well advised to divide your estate equally between yourself and your wife so that you each benefit from the £223 000 nil-rate band. Whichever of you died first could then take advantage by passing assets of that value to your children. This would then leave the balance to the spouse free of IHT under the surviving spouse exemption (*see* Question 73).

You may also wish to consider making annual lifetime transfers of up to £3000 in total, which are exempt from tax, and possibly further lifetime gifts, which would be exempt so long as you survive for 7 years after making the gift.

There are more sophisticated schemes of estate planning that could help you and you would be well advised to discuss this with a professional adviser.

▲ Question 73: Inheritance Tax: surviving spouse exemption

I have a considerable estate made up largely of property, stocks and shares. I want to leave these to my wife in my will but am worried in case she will be charged Inheritance Tax (IHT).

Do not worry. Where property is left by will to a surviving spouse there is no IHT charged on that gift. The tax may, however, be chargeable if you were to leave gifts to another party.

Please remember, however, that your wife, if she survives you, may be chargeable to the full amount of IHT when she in her turn dies, and it may be wise for you to obtain specialist estate-planning advice in order to minimize the possible incidence of IHT at some future time. *See* Question 72.

▲ Question 74: Tax on sale of land

I own a piece of land adjoining my house and am considering selling it. However, I am worried that I might have to pay some sort of development tax on this. Can you tell me if this applies? Could I be charged Capital Gains Tax (CGT)?

Development land tax was abolished some years ago and therefore there can only be a liability for CGT in certain cases. However, if the total area of land adjoining your house is less than about 2 acres, you are unlikely to be charged CGT on the sale. If the total area of land is over that extent, you could have a CGT liability but this would depend on the proportionate cost of the land in the first place. In any event, this would be reduced by the indexation relief, by re-basing and by the normal annual exemption (for 1997/98 this was £6500) provided that you have held it over several years.

▲ Question 75: Capital Gains Tax on private house sale

I have been claiming relief from income tax in respect of part of the running costs of my home. The Inspector has for some years allowed one-quarter of these costs.

I have now been told that, because of this, I may be liable for Capital Gains Tax (CGT) on the sale of this house. Is this right?

No. Unless you have any part of the house set aside **exclusively** for practice purposes there will be no charge to CGT on such a sale.

Even if you were to have some part of the house set aside exclusively for your practice and a capital gain did arise on the sale, if you bought a replacement house and practised from there you would be able to claim roll-over relief. If you sold the house upon retirement it would almost certainly rank for CGT retirement relief, provided that it was sold within 12 months of retirement. This period can be extended if there are difficulties in selling the house.

There is, in practice, very little prospect of you actually having CGT to pay on a sale of your private house under these circumstances.

10

Wives, Spouses and Families

▲ Question 76: Married man's allowance

I am a married doctor and my taxable income is about £40 000 per annum. My wife is a schoolteacher earning about £20 000 per annum. Up to 1990 we elected for separate assessment but since wives are now taxed separately from their husbands, such an election is no longer necessary.

I see from my tax assessment that my married man's allowance has now gone down to £268.50 from the previous figure of £1720. This seems to be an awfully big drop. Has the Inspector got the figures right?

You are aware that since 1990 husbands and wives have been considered, for most practical purposes, to be separate people for tax purposes and there is no need whatever for you to make any further elections. You will be taxed separately without any further action on your part.

For the 1998/99 year, you would receive the basic personal allowance of £4195. In addition, you will also be entitled to the married couple's allowance of £1900. You can in fact elect which of you is to receive this but the amount will not change and there is no advantage either way.

With regard to the amount of the allowance, you may well be confusing the allowance and the actual tax benefit. For 1998/99, the married couple's allowance is £1900. This was reduced to a maximum of 15% so that in tax terms this would represent a benefit of only £285. This 15% rate will fall to 10% from 6 April 1999.

If either of you have any investment income, this will be taxed directly upon the spouse concerned.

▲ Question 77: Wife with outside employment

I am a married GP and pay my wife a salary for telephone-answering, reception, secretarial duties and so on, which are performed at our house where I frequently receive patients.

Now that our young children have started school my wife has more time available and is proposing to take an outside job during the day, for which she will be paid about £8000 per annum. I understand that because of this I should stop paying my wife a salary. Is this right?

No, it is not. It is a common misconception that where a wife has outside employment which will more than cover her personal income tax allowance, the salary paid by the husband should cease. This is not the case. What is more important to remember is that, in circumstances such as these, there can be no possible loss of benefit to the family unit. The worst that can happen is that you will transfer a tax liability from yourself to your wife. You should, however, ensure that the salary you pay your wife remains below the Class 1 National Insurance contributions threshold, otherwise the charging of National Insurance contributions may outweigh any tax advantages.

In addition, it may be that at some time in the future your wife will cease employment for some reason. The salary that you pay to her will then again become tax-efficient. If you were to cease paying it for a period, the Inspector of Taxes could decide that it was not essential for your practice and when you choose to claim again, refuse to allow this.

In addition, if your wife was to cease being your employee, you would lose the opportunity of other claims arising from her employment by you, such as wife's pension contributions, medical insurance premiums and so on.

▲ Question 78: Payment of wife's salary

For some years I have been claiming a salary for my wife through my own practice expenses claim. This has not actually been paid by me but has been adjusted by our accountant through the accounts.

I have now heard that it should be necessary to actually pay this money across. Can you tell me if this is true?

Yes. What you are talking about has in the past merely been a paper transaction and the Inland Revenue would be quite within their rights in refusing to accept this as allowable expenditure.

While it may now be too late to put right what has happened in previous years, as soon as possible you should immediately bring into force some form of physical transfer of funds between the two of you. Ideally, this should be a monthly cheque drawn on your own bank account and paid into a private account in the name of your wife.

If you do not have separate accounts, or operate a joint account, you may wish to open, say, a building society account in your wife's name and deposit the money there. Alternatively, you could draw a cash cheque each month, for the actual amount of the salary, marking the counterfoil clearly 'wife's salary'.

It cannot be too strongly emphasized that the failure to pay a salary to your wife and, if necessary, be in a position to produce evidence to the Inland Revenue that you have done so, could quite easily mean that the salary will be disallowed. This may be even more far-reaching in its effect as it could also lead to the disallowance of other amounts paid as a result of this salary, such as pension premiums, medical sickness policies and so on.

▲ Question 79: Married women doctors

I am a married woman doctor and hence am unable to claim a 'wife's salary' as can my male colleagues. This seems a little unfair. What can I do to put myself on the same footing as my male partners?

You can of course only be on the same footing if all of you genuinely pay a salary to a spouse or other suitable person for genuine services in assisting your practice.

If you are not incurring any such expenditure or have no need to do so, then you would be unable to justify a claim and it would not be right for you to make one. But if you have a husband who deals with telephone-answering and similar services on your behalf from your own house on behalf of the patients, there is no reason why you should not pay him a salary. However, the likelihood is that your husband will already be paying tax at a high rate. If you were to pay him a salary you will have to be careful to ensure that you are not merely transferring to him taxable income upon which he would have to pay tax at a higher rate than that at which you are obtaining relief. You also need to consider the input of the employer's National Insurance on any salary paid to him, which would certainly negate any tax advantages.

If you have any suitable children of the right age who are able to perform such services, again this is no reason why you should not pay them a salary and claim for it. However, a salary must actually be paid and you must be capable of producing evidence both of payment and of the duties that they perform.

However, if you are unable to benefit from paying a spouse a salary then so long as your partners are paying their wives out of their personal funds and claiming the tax relief on the salary in their personal expenses claims rather than the wives' salaries being paid through the accounts, you will not suffer any loss of income. You would merely be obtaining less tax relief than your partners.

▲ Question 80: Wives' salaries in partnership

In my partnership we have, for many years, paid salaries to the partners' wives out of the partnership bank account. We have now taken on a young unmarried doctor who objects to this procedure and does not see why he should pay a share of the salaries paid to other partners' wives. How can we get round this problem?

The views of your new partner are both understandable and justifiable.

It is now standard practice for GPs in partnership to pay their wives personally and not out of partnership funds. By this means, the salaries paid to the wives can be claimed with their own personal practice expenses rather than through the partnership accounts. This avoids the problem raised by the inclusion in partnerships of women or unmarried doctors who may have no facility for paying salaries to their wives. Even if a partnership consists entirely of married male doctors, it is usually best to set a precedent by paying these salaries personally and ensuring that the problem cannot arise in the future.

There are also more significant advantages; for example, a doctor may quite properly wish to pension his wife. If he does so and pays the pension contributions himself, while the salary is paid out of partnership funds, he may find the pension contributions are disallowed on the grounds that they have not been paid by the employer. With the wives being presumably of different ages and attracting differing premiums, it would be most inequitable to pass all these premiums through the partnership accounts. For similar reasons, a doctor could find that contributions to medical insurance policies are also disallowed.

It is strongly recommended that wives' salaries be paid personally by the doctors concerned rather than out of partnership funds.

▲ Question 81: Wives' pensions

I have employed my wife in my practice for some years and a salary has always been paid to her and allowed by the Inland Revenue.

I have now been told that it will be beneficial for me to subscribe to a pension scheme for my wife. Do you agree and how much is the maximum I can contribute? How should the premium be claimed?

The payment of pension premiums in respect of the working wife of a GP, deriving from a salary paid by the GP for work in his practice, is extremely tax-efficient as it will be allowed in full against his top rate of tax.

The amount you pay cannot really be determined by yourself but is calculated by the insurance company to whom you make the payments. This is done on the principle that you can only purchase sufficient pension, to accord with Inland Revenue rules, as will give your wife on her own retirement a pension not exceeding two-thirds of her final salary.

It is strongly recommended that all GPs make such pension provisions for their wife; not only do they obtain full tax relief on their premiums but, on retirement, the pension will be treated as earned income in the hands of the wife. It is likely that this will be fully covered by her own personal allowance, thus ensuring that the pension is received entirely tax free.

Again, it is recommended that you approach companies with a proven record in this field and obtain at least two quotations. If necessary these should be examined by your accountant or other independent advisers.

It should also be ensured that the insurance company obtains for you a notice of agreement from the superannuation funds office that the pension scheme is acceptable to them.

Relief for these premiums should not be claimed through the personal income tax return of the doctor concerned. They are, in effect, an expense of running his practice and should be included in his own personal practice expenses claim, in the same way that he claims his wife's salary (*see* Question 78).

▲ Question 82: Medical insurance policies

My wife and I subscribe to BUPA and I wonder if there is any way we can obtain tax relief for the amounts we pay each year?

In your own case, there is no way in which you can obtain direct tax relief for what are in effect medical insurance policies. Certainly they are not an allowable deduction in your own claim for practice expenses.

However, if you employ your wife in your practice and she is accepted by the Inland Revenue as a genuine employee (*see* Question 78), you may include the proportion of the premiums that represents those on behalf of your wife in your own claim for practice expenses, in the same way as you claim her salary and, possibly, pension contributions and so on (*see* Question 78).

So long as your wife is not treated as a higher-paid employee (earning over £8500 p.a.), the cost to you to provide these benefits for her will not be taxed upon her.

▲ Question 83: Tax in year of marriage

I am getting married shortly and my future wife will continue to work. Can you tell me exactly what tax allowances we will be allowed and how this will affect our tax position?

On your marriage you will immediately commence to receive the married couple's allowance (*see* Question 76) as opposed to the single man's allowance you have previously been receiving. If you marry during the course of a tax year, you will be granted a proportion of the additional relief for that year only.

11

Pensions, Superannuation and Retirement

▲ Question 84: 24-hour retirement and abatement of pension

I am shortly coming up to retirement age and I hope to retire just after by 60th birthday in about 6 months time.

However, I wish to carry on in practice and understand I cannot do this without losing my pension. Is this right?

Until recently, doctors could indeed retire and take their pension, being immediately re-engaged the following day. This was known as '24-hour' retirement. Since 1995, however, the rules have changed somewhat and a doctor wishing to be re-engaged, in his own or any other practice, is required to leave practice for at least one month.

If you retire after age 60, the abatement rule will not normally come into operation and you can receive your practice earnings, at whatever proportion you choose, as well as your pension.

You will be well advised before retirement to obtain from the Superannuations Fund Office an outline of your pension and lump sum entitlement. This will enable you to plan for the future and see exactly how much pension and practice income you will need to meet your anticipated living costs.

Before agreeing this step you should discuss the matter with your partners, who will have the problem of deciding exactly who is to fill the gap caused by your reduction in working hours, if indeed that is your intention.

▲ Question 85: Continuing superannuation contributions

I have recently retired from the NHS at 65 years of age but I am continuing in practice following partial retirement. I have not purchased any added years or made private pension contributions but I would like to continue paying contributions under the NHS scheme. Am I obliged to stop paying these contributions at the age of 65 years?

No, you are not. You can contribute to a maximum contribution under the NHS scheme of 45 years' service, both earned and purchased at age 65 years, but you will not be allowed to purchase total service over 45 years. If you therefore continue in practice you can pay these contributions up to a maximum of 45 years but you must stop paying once you have reached that maximum or have to retire fully at the age of 70 years.

▲ Question 86: Tax allowance for superannuation

How should superannuation contributions be claimed for income tax purposes? I am a GP in practice but can find no reference to superannuation in the accounts produced by our accountant. I have asked the accountant and he says that he was not aware that we had paid any, although quite clearly it is deducted from our fees each quarter by the Health Authority (HA).

The proper manner in which superannuation contributions should be allowed for tax purposes is on an actual year, rather than the preceding-year, basis.

What may have happened here is that your accountant has not studied the information presented by the HA quarterly statement and is unaware that these contributions are being paid. If the net fees are merely shown in your accounts, without the superannuation being added back, the effect will be that, although they will be allowed for tax purposes, this will be on the current year rather than the more beneficial actual-year basis (assuming your accounting year-end is other than 31 March).

If there are differential superannuation contributions by the partners, which is extremely likely, not only because you may have different seniority awards but also because some of the partners might be buying added years, considerable inequity between the partners can result from this incorrect treatment.

You should instruct your accountant to design the accounts in the prescribed manner, so that the gross fee income of the practice can be clearly seen. Superannuation contributions should not be shown as an item of expense in the annual accounts; they are not properly an expense of running the practice but a payment for purchase of eventual pension benefit. As such, they should be charged directly to the partners concerned in their own capital or current accounts and tax relief should be claimed on an actual-year basis through the medium of the personal income tax returns of the doctor concerned.

▲ Question 87: Purchase of added years

I am 49 years of age and have been a GP since I was aged 30. It seems that if I retire at 60 I will not get a particularly high pension and wonder if I can do anything about this. Can you suggest ways in which I can increase my pension, possibly by buying further years of service?

Discounting any possible credit you might receive for years of working in the hospital service, you have already completed 19 years of service as a GP principal. You have, counting round years only, a further 11 years to go until retirement at 60 or 16 years at age 65. This is a potential superannuable service of 30 years, compared with the maximum 40 years at age 60 to qualify for a full pension.

The maximum contribution you can make to the NHS pension scheme is 15%, which, taking into consideration your basic 6% contribution, leaves only a 9% margin payable under the added years scheme. At your next birthday you will be age 50, at which age each added year will cost 2.25%, so you could purchase only 4 such years to bring you up to your maximum 15% contribution, assuming you are proposing to retire at age 60.

You would be strongly advised, if you decide to purchase added years, to do this under the 'age 60' rather than the 'age 65' scales as under the latter scheme there are certain actuarial disadvantages should you ultimately decide to retire before 65 years of age.

It may be that you would be better advised to make contributions to a private pension scheme, renouncing your tax relief and getting a full tax refund on your private premium. *See* Question 89.

There is also a facility for purchase of Free-Standing Additional Voluntary Contributions, which are a type of private added years and subject to similar restrictions. *See* Question 96.

▲ Question 88: Private pension contributions: non-NHS income

I am a member of a partnership that receives some private fees from patients. All of the partnership income is pooled for division.

I am 48 years of age and have now been approached by somebody who wishes to sell me a pension policy saying that I can use my share of this private income and pay contributions on that amount. Is this correct?

No. It is not strictly correct. This is a common misconception but not the true position. Provisions for the granting of tax relief on doctors' superannuation contributions, both NHS and private, are set out in Inland Revenue Extra-Statutory Concession A9.

The position is that you should obtain details of your actual NHS contributions in any year of assessment. These should then be 'grossed-up' by multiplying by a factor of 100/6, in order to arrive at your superannuable income for that year of assessment. Thus, if between 6 April 1996 and 5 April 1997 you paid NHS standard superannuation contributions of £2400, this 'grossed-up' gives a figure of £40 000. Added years' contributions should be ignored for the purpose of this calculation.

It is then necessary to compare that figure with the actual Schedule D assessment, or your share of the partnership tax assessment. If the Schedule D figure is greater, you can then pay personal pension contributions up to an amount of 25% on the difference. The percentage of net relevant earnings payable depends upon your age, varying from 17.5% before age 35, up to 40% for taxpayers aged 61 years and over.

If therefore, on that basis, the Schedule D assessment was, say £42 000, this would leave a margin over and above the NHS superannuable income of £2000, upon which you would be entitled to obtain tax relief on premiums of £500 (£2000 at 25%).

This is the only manner in which tax relief can be granted on premiums under this heading; the example shown above is the exception rather than the rule. In most cases of purely NHS practice, there proves to be little or no margin available upon which such a claim can be made.

▲ Question 89: Renunciation of NHS tax relief

I joined the NHS rather late in life and have been advised that I cannot buy sufficient added years of service to make an appreciable difference to my pension. I understand I can opt out of tax relief on my NHS contributions in favour of a private scheme. Is this correct and how do I go about it?

Yes; it can provide an excellent scheme but you must bear in mind that you will be paying two sets of contributions (the NHS scheme and the private scheme) and getting tax relief on only one. A great advantage of this scheme is that you can pay these contributions out of capital if this is available, rather than from income, although you must have sufficient taxable income against which the relief can be granted.

The tax relief that you lose on your NHS contributions can be a factor. For instance, if a doctor was paying, say, £2400 per annum in standard NHS contributions with a top tax rate of 40%, he would lose £960 in direct tax relief. On the other hand, the relief he would gain on his private pension contributions would be very much higher and would ensure that he would enjoy a greatly enhanced pension at retirement.

If you are buying added years you would also have to renounce the tax relief on those contributions, which in effect usually makes the scheme uneconomic for those doctors buying added years (*see* Question 87).

In order to make the scheme worthwhile, you would be well advised to contribute the maximum you can. This can prove expensive; a GP aged 58 years with net relevant earnings of £40 000 for

1997/98 could contribute 35% of that amount, or £14 000, upon which he would attract tax relief at 40% of £5600, reducing the net cost to £8400, to which must be added the lost tax relief on his NHS contributions.

You should initially discuss this with your accountant or other independent financial adviser, who will both be able to look at your particular case and advise which policies are the most beneficial for you.

▲ Question 90: Taxation of GP pension

I shall be retiring from practice at the age of 61 years in a few months' time. I am very worried about income tax on my pension and lump-sum payment. Can you explain how this will be dealt with and will I be able to claim any expenses against my pension? I have always claimed for my car, house and so on during my working life.

Firstly, your lump-sum payment will not attract any form of taxation whatsoever. It is tax-free, although you will of course be taxed on any income that arises directly from the investment of that money.

Your pension will be paid to you each month by the Paymaster General's office and will be taxed by operation of the PAYE system as if you were an employee. You will receive a pension paid monthly; in other words, one-twelfth of your annual pension entitlement at the end of each month, from which income tax will be deducted in accordance with the code number that you are given. This coding will reflect the level of your personal tax allowances. There will be no deduction for National Insurance.

It will not be possible for you to claim any expenses on the lines you indicate against this pension. The items you quote are expenses of running your medical practice and, as you are no longer in practice, you will presumably have no medical fees against which the expenses are incurred. If you were to continue to do some medical work, such as locums and so on, or if you continue in practice for any reason, any such expenditure could be claimed against income earned only from that source, but not against your pension. The same principle applies to medical subscriptions.

▲ Question 91: Cessation of practice: tax position

I am aged 62 years and a sole practitioner. I am considering retiring on 30 June 1998, which will be my birthday and I should like to know what the tax implications of this will be.

The answer to this really depends upon the date to which your practice accounts are drawn up. If one assumes that they are drawn up to 30 June annually, with a further full year up to the date of your retirement, you will be liable for all tax on earnings up to the date of your retirement.

If, therefore, under the new current year basis of assessment, you realized a profit of, say £40 000 in the year to 30 June 1997, then this would be taxable in the year 1997/98. You would be required to pay two substantial payments on account of this liability on 31 January and 31 July 1998, with a balancing payment on 31 July 1999. You will see therefore that both the second payment on account and the balancing payment (or refund, if appropriate) will be made after the date of your retirement.

If one further assumes that you realize a profit of £45 000 in your final year of practice, up to 30 June 1998, this will be assessed in the tax year 1998/99, of which tax will be payable on 31 January and 31 July 1999, with a balancing payment (or repayment) on 31 January 2000.

It will be seen that there is likely to be a substantial tax liability following your departure from the practice. You would be as well to obtain an estimate of that amount, which would enable you to put funds aside to ensure the liability is met. You may well be able to utilize your overlap relief which would have originated during the change from the preceding year to the current year basis.

▲ Question 92: Retirement from practice

I am a member of a medical partnership and have funds invested both in the surgery and in other assets. How can I realize these when I retire?

Firstly, the matter should be set out fully in your partnership deed (*see* Question 34). A well drawn-up deed should set out, in full and clear detail, the provisions for partners' retirement and for withdrawing their own capital funds from the practice.

To be as brief as possible, you should expect to be paid the share of your equity in the surgery premises (*see* Question 40) and the balances on your capital and current accounts. These represent your share of the partnership fixed assets and working capital of the practice, as represented by the current assets (such as cash, debtors and so on) less creditors, at any given time.

▲ Question 93: Retirement at 50

I understand a scheme has been introduced for GPs to retire at age 50 and take their pension. I am in general practice; I do not enjoy this very much and would like to turn either to another branch of medicine or something different altogether. I am aged 47. Should I take my pension at age 50?

This is a personal question and one which in the last analysis can only be decided by the doctor concerned. Those GPs who retire at age 50 will find that their pension is substantially reduced. The proportion of this will depend on how long the GP has been a member of the NHS pension scheme and how much his accumulated career earnings will generate as pension.

Many doctors will be considering this option and will inevitably come up against the problem that their pension will clearly not be sufficient to allow them to live in the manner to which they have become accustomed. It will be necessary to take on other work, provided this is available.

This is a question you should consider with your own professional advisors, firstly obtaining details of your likely pension entitlement to date.

▲ Question 94: Opting out of the NHS superannuation scheme

I understand that I can, if necessary, stop making contributions to the NHS superannuation scheme. Is this correct and will it be of benefit to me as I have been told I can put the whole of the amount I save into a private pension plan?

It is correct that you can opt out of the NHS superannuation scheme (NHSSS) altogether.

However, bear in mind that, together with your own contributions, the Government makes a further contribution to the scheme and you would lose the benefit of this if you were to opt out entirely. Any benefit from contributions to a private scheme would be based upon your own contributions only.

The NHSSS also has several benefits not entirely and exclusively connected to pensions. There is an attractive lump sum on retirement, together with earlier possible benefits for sickness, death in service, widows and families' benefit and so on. Furthermore, the

NHSSS is an index-linked scheme and the benefits of contributing to it should not lightly be thrown away.

Except in very exceptional circumstances, it is difficult to envisage a situation in which a GP would be well advised to opt out of the scheme entirely. This is a different and far-reaching decision, and quite different from merely opting out of the tax relief on NHS contributions (*see* Question 88).

▲ Question 95: Sale of surgery share on retirement

I shall be retiring from practice shortly and currently own a share of a surgery that is mortgaged with the GP Finance Corporation. The surgery has not been valued but I think that its present value is £800 000. The outstanding mortgage is £500 000. When I retire, will I be paid the quarter share of the total value of the property and will I have to repay the mortgage? When will I be able to get the money?

The usual position when doctors retire or leave a practice for any reason is that they will agree to be paid their appropriate share of the equity in the surgery only. For your purpose this works out as shown in Figure 6.

	£
Total valuation	800 000
Less outstanding mortgage	500 000
	300 000
One-quarter share	75 000

Figure 6: Share of equity on retirement.

Subject to your partners agreeing the value of the surgery, therefore, and the outstanding capital on the mortgage being an accurate figure, you could reasonably expect to receive £75 000 as your share in the equity in this surgery. Your outstanding share of the GP Finance Corporation mortgage would be passed on either to the continuing partners, if they purchase your share, or possibly to an incoming partner. Your partnership deed should set down precisely the means and timing for this money to be paid over to you. It would be normal for interest to be paid from the date of your retirement. For Capital Gains Tax reasons (*see* Question 41) it would be advisable for such a sale to take place not more than 1 year after the date of your retirement.

▲ Question 96: Additional voluntary contributions

I am a GP aged 51 years. I would like to make additional pension contributions but do not want to subscribe to the added years scheme as I do not want to commit myself to making payments each year until I retire. Nor do I want to make the substantial contributions that would be necessary to justify renunciation of the tax relief on my NHS contributions. Is there any other way that I can enhance my eventual pension benefit?

I recommend that you consider making Free-Standing Additional Voluntary Contributions (FSAVCs). Since 1989 a GP has been able to pay into a personal pension scheme a maximum of 9%. This will bring your total contributions on your NHS superannuable income up from 6% (standard contribution) to a maximum of 15%.

FSAVCs have several advantages: (a) they can be stopped and started as one wishes; (b) one is not committing oneself to a large payment each year and (c) they qualify for basic-rate tax relief at source.

If a GP is entitled to tax relief above the basic rate, this will be granted through his annual income tax assessment.

However, FSAVCs are subject to market forces; unlike added years the eventual benefit does not entirely reflect total career earnings. In addition, the eventual benefit can be taken only as a pension and not as a lump sum. GPs who have already acquired a total career entitlement of 36⅔ years, including added years purchased, are unable to participate in the scheme. This is to ensure that GPs do not receive, with their pension, an entitlement above the Inland Revenue maximum of two-thirds final 'salary'.

12

Investments and Finance

▲ Question 97: Investments for children

My children, who are aged 12 and 14 years, have just been left some money by an elderly relative. Each of these legacies should amount to around £5000 for each child. Neither of the children has any other source of income and I should like to know how I should best invest this so that they are not liable for income tax.

A great number of bank and building society accounts are open to children and others who are not taxpayers. Many banks and building societies offer relatively attractive rates of interest, as does the Investment Account with the National Savings Bank. From time to time there are particularly attractive offers, for instance, through National Savings schemes which guarantee a generous rate of interest and are exempt from tax. You would be well advised to shop around for the best rate on offer and ensure that any interest accumulation on the amount is paid without deduction of tax.

▲ Question 98: Tax-free investments

I have recently taken partial retirement from the NHS and have received a substantial lump sum. I do not want to generate additional income that would be subject to tax at a high rate and wonder if there are means by which I could invest this money, so that it would grow but not produce a taxable income?

You would be well advised, provided that you have adequate income to cover your known living expenses, not to invest funds of this nature in investments that will generate unwanted income and would also be subject to a high rate of tax. You therefore need to consider either investments producing capital growth or those generating a return that are exempt from income tax.

There are several schemes now available by which this could be done. You could, for instance, consider the latest issue of National Savings certificates (*see* Question 102), which offer a reasonable, if unexciting, return which is non-taxable. There are also index-linked National Savings Certificates, which you should consider.

Tax-Exempt Special Savings Accounts (TESSAs) are on offer from most banks and building societies. These offer a varying rate of interest, equivalent to prevailing bank interest rates but which, up to a limit, are exempt from all taxation. Under these schemes, the income cannot be drawn until the date of maturity, normally 5 years, but you should consider these as a priority. TESSAs will only be available up to April 1999.

A further limited source is the ordinary amount at the National Savings Bank, upon which tax is not payable on interest up to £70 for each individual.

Your financial adviser would be able to recommend investments producing capital growth against which you could offset your annual Capital Gains Tax exemption of £6500 on realization.

You might also consider a Personal Equity Plan, *see* Question 99.

▲ Question 99: PEPs

I understand that it is possible to invest in PEPs and obtain tax relief on them. Is this the case and how do I go about this?

Personal Equity Plans (PEPs) were introduced in the 1980s as an encouragement to saving and up to certain limits are exempt from all income tax and Capital Gains Tax in the hands of the holders.

It is not quite true to say that you can obtain tax relief on these investments. Investment in PEPs will not reduce your overall tax liability, nor will it reduce any existing Capital Gains Tax liability. What it will do is ensure that you have no liability for tax on any interest, dividends, or capital gains which might result from your ownership of a PEP.

At the moment, you can invest up to £6000 per annum in a 'general' PEP, i.e. one in which investment in a multiplicity of funds are made. You can also invest an additional £3000 p.a. in a single company PEP. This single company can change from year to year but up to the maximum must be invested in the same company in a single tax year.

It will be seen, therefore, that a couple can invest a total of £18 000 in a single tax year, all of this resulting in no tax whatever on any income or capital gains which might result.

It is fair to add that the Chancellor of the Exchequer has announced that he will remove the tax beneficial status of PEPs (and TESSAs) from 6 April 1999. Any PEPs held at that date can be retained and their tax exempt status will continue. Any such tax exempt savings after that date will be through the new Individual Savings Accounts (ISAs).

▲ Question 100: Mid-term endowment policies

I understand that I can buy life policies that have been partly paid up. How do I do this and is it a good investment?

This is an extremely good investment provided all the issues are understood. We are talking here of the acquisition of mid-term endowment policies, which will have been taken out at some time and discarded for reasons best known to the insured.

These policies do come on to the market from time to time; they are offered at auction and can result in extremely generous yields.

For instance, a policy which has, say, 5 years to maturity can be acquired at a negotiated capital sum; the purchaser/investor continues to be responsible for the premiums and receives the benefit and terminal bonus at the end of the term. While these cannot be accurately forecast, it is reasonable to anticipate yields of an estimated 10–12%, which is far more than will be realized from a conventional investment at the present time.

▲ Question 101: Inheritance Tax exemption

My husband and I have come into possession of a large amount of money due to gifts and proceeds from estates, which we do not really need and we would like to give some of this away to our family. How do we go about this without incurring any Inheritance Tax (IHT) liability?

There is at the moment an annual IHT exemption of £3000 for each person, where the husband and wife are treated separately. A couple could therefore give away in a single year £6000. Furthermore, if they make no gifts in the previous year they can carry forward that £6000 exemption to the following year, giving a total of £12 000 in all.

It is also possible to give away £250 each in separate gifts over and above that limit. You can also make additional gifts in anticipation of marriage and there are set levels laid down for parents, grandparents and other relatives.

Apart from this, you can make 'potentially-exempt transfers' without limit. In those cases, if the donor survives for 7 years, the gift falls out of charge to IHT and no liability arises. There is a tapering level of charge if the donor dies within that 7-year period.

If you have inherited the legacies within the last 2 years, you could seek to make a Deed of Family Arrangement whereby you effectively rewrite the relevant will to leave that portion of the estate to a person of your choice, thus, for example, passing the money direct to your children from the deceased. All the beneficiaries of the will have to give their consent to such a Deed and you would need to discuss this with your solicitor.

▲ Question 102: National Savings

I have no funds invested in National Savings and pay tax at the top rate. I understand these are extremely tax efficient. Do you think I should invest in National Savings?

National Savings are a limited investment and the current certificate on offer is the 45th issue, which at present offers a rate of interest of 5.35%, provided the certificates are held for 5 years. For a 40% taxpayer, this gives a gross equivalent yield of 8.3%. This is higher than is currently obtainable in most other investments.

The minimum purchase is £100 and the maximum holding is £10 000.

You can, of course, hold the maximum in earlier issues. National Savings Certificates can be bought at any Post Office and many branches of the major banks. Also currently available is the 12th issue of the index-linked issue, which again can be bought in multiples of £100 up to £10 000. The return, which again is entirely tax free, is calculated by the rate of inflation, as measured by the Retail Prices Index. To this factor is added a further 2.5% for certificates held to maturity (5 years).

If you are adventurous and wish to gamble the amounts of annual interest, Premium Savings Bonds are also available, up to a maximum holding of £20 000. Any prize that might be won is entirely free of all taxes.

▲ Question 103: Saving through life assurance

I understand that I can save money through investment in a life assurance policy. Is this true and how do I go about it?

If you wish to save by this means, the best method of doing so would be with an endowment insurance policy. Tax relief on life assurance premiums was abolished in 1984, so, apart from policies in existence before that date, you will obtain no tax relief on such premiums.

If you are proposing to invest by these means you should check those insurance companies offering the best record of growth. There are some companies, for instance, that do not offer a commission charge and some of these consequently may have a better record of growth than some commission-paying companies.

Such a policy will be taken out over a fixed number of years, say 10 or 20, and you must accept that your premiums should be paid for the full term. If you discontinue the premiums or decide to surrender the policies before the maturity date, you could lose much of the investment already made.

Endowment policies can be 'without profits', in which case at the end of the term you will receive back exactly the amount for which your life is insured. This would also be paid in the event of your prior death. Alternatively, you could take out a 'with profits' policy, to which will be added a bonus reflecting the success of the company's investment policy over the period. Premiums on such a 'with profits' policy would be higher than on a 'without profits' policy. A major benefit of 'with profits' policies is the terminal bonus which is an encouragement to continue the policy to final maturity.

You can take out these policies directly with an insurance company but you may prefer to do it through your accountant, an insurance broker, or your bank, who will be able to advise you on the best policies available. Make sure any advice you obtain is from a company or business registered under the Financial Services Acts.

13

Doctors and the Accountancy Profession

▲ Question 104: Personal or partnership accountant?

I will shortly be joining a partnership and it has been suggested that I should use the partnership accountant. I already have an accountant of my own with whom I am extremely satisfied. Should I continue to use him?

Firstly, it must be said that you are perfectly free to choose your own professional adviser and it would be quite wrong to attempt to deprive you of this right. However, there can be advantages in using the partnership accountant to deal with your personal affairs. It tends to minimize cost and time, although again this depends on the efficiency and speciality of the various accountants involved.

On balance, you will usually find that it will be more beneficial for you in many ways for your partnership accountant to deal with your personal financial affairs but in the last analysis it should be your own decision and no one else's!

▲ Question 105: Accountancy fees

I am very concerned at the amount of accountancy fees my practice is paying. We are a partnership of six doctors and our fees have increased in recent years to such a degree that we are now wondering if we should change to a smaller and less expensive firm of accountants. Is this wise?

It is impossible to say without any further information if you should change accountants, but if the present accountants are doing a good job for you it would be better to retain their services. Indeed, the mere fact of changing could cost you money, particularly in the first year, if a new accountant wishes to introduce an entirely new system of accounting.

Accountants employ able and qualified staff, many of them experienced in the affairs of GPs; and the time used by these accountants in dealing with your affairs is likely to be lengthy and expensive. It is impossible to lay down 'hard-and-fast' guidelines as to exact fee levels but you should not change accountants unless you are sure that the new firm will offer you at least as good or better service at a reduced cost.

Before deciding to change accountants for the sake of fee levels, you should ask yourselves whether you are doing all you can yourselves to help to reduce them. For instance, an adequate system of bookkeeping should greatly reduce the work your accountant is required to do, and hence his fees (*see* Question 2).

As a general rule accountancy fees for GP partnerships, including work on the partners' personal affairs, should not exceed £1000 per partner, with normal regional variations.

If you feel strongly on the matter, ask for competitive quotations from reputable and specialist firms. The BMA now has its own accountancy arm, BMA Professional Services Ltd. The Association of Independent Specialist Medical Accountants (Tel: 01424 730345) can recommend specialist firms who have achieved AISMA's stringent entry conditions.

▲ Question 106: Changing accountants

We have been with our accountants for many years but it is becoming apparent that they do not understand our affairs, particularly in connection with our new cost-rent project and buying added years of superannuation. After a great deal of thought we have now finally decided to change our accountants and have found a firm specializing in this field. How do we approach that firm and is there any difficulty in changing from one firm to another?

Both the items you mention are unique to the medical profession and would be understood without undue difficulty by an accountant specializing in this field. If you have identified the firm you would like to engage, presumably having satisfied yourselves that they are the specialists you require, your best course would be to approach them and ask one of their senior members to come and visit the partnership for a discussion. It is usually far better if you can speak with the person who will be dealing with your affairs and ask him some of the questions that have been troubling you.

Firstly, try to ensure that he is a specialist. Ask him how many practices he deals with and ask him certain leading questions concerning GPs' accounts. For instance, has he got a copy of the Statement of Fees and Allowances (Red Book) and does he understand how it works? Does he know about such matters as (a) the claiming of item of service fees; (b) average levels of income; (c) the cost-rent scheme; (d) added years; (e) superannuation; (f) seniority and post-graduate education allowances; together with all the numerous items which are part of the GP's financial package? If he is unable to answer these questions it is unlikely that he is the accountant you are looking for.

Ask him who will be dealing with your affairs; try to ensure that his firm has a specialist department dealing with GPs and that his staff are also conversant with this type of work. If he wants to attract your business he will not be adverse to visiting you, meeting the partners and answering questions of this nature.

Provided that this procedure is satisfactory, you should then write to that firm instructing them to act for you and advising them that you have also written to your previous accountants.

It will be necessary for your new accountants to write to the retiring accountant asking for the routine clearance, which will enable them to act for you. This is in accordance with accountants' professional ethics and a courtesy that is invariably carried out. Provided there is no such objection, the old accountants would write to the new accountants, giving them the information for which they ask, at the same time sending to them such papers as they require.

It is normally a good idea on occasions such as this to agree that the old accountants will settle all outstanding matters, including partnership tax liabilities, up to a certain year and the new accountants will deal with them thereafter. If there are any years outstanding it is usually a good idea for the original accountants to settle these as the process of handing these over in mid-stream is usually expensive and rarely satisfactory.

▲ Question 107: Finding an accountant

My partners and I have thought for some time about changing accountants and we are well aware of the need to have a specialist dealing with our affairs. However, this is easier said than done; how do we find such a specialist accountant as we have no knowledge whatever of that profession? Our old accountant has acted for us for many years and was the accountant for the practice when all of us joined.

The task of finding such an accountant is by no means as difficult now as it was a few years ago. Accountants' rules on advertising have now been relaxed and it is possible for firms with a proven speciality in this field to make their presence known to GPs at large.

In addition, specialist firms are frequently invited to contribute financial articles to medical newspapers and you can therefore look through these journals to see which firms have the expertise to contribute regular articles of this nature.

Within the last few years there has been set up for the first time a body catering for specialist medical accountants who are independent firms accredited with work for GPs. Doctors have the assurance of knowing that the work of member firms has been inspected by known specialists. They work to a Charter which can be supplied on request. GPs interested should contact Liz Densley at the Association of Independent Specialist Medical Accountants (AISMA) – Tel 01424 730345 – for further information.

Also widely active in the field is BMA Professional Services Ltd, a wholly owned subsidiary of the British Medical Association which offers specialist accountancy and taxation services. BMA members and others interested should initially contact BMAPS on 0171 383 6743.

▲ Question 108: Bookkeeping

My practice has always had its account books written up by our accountant who visits the practice once a week or so and keeps the books up to date. This is now costing us a lot of money and I wonder if we can find any way round this? Should the accountant be doing this at all?

No, he should not. It is indeed expensive to have a professional accountant doing this work. He will charge you a fee plus VAT for dealing with it and you will be unable to obtain any direct reimbursement for his fees. You would be well advised either to ask your practice manager to deal with the bookkeeping or, if she is unwilling or unable to do so, in a sufficiently large practice, engage a specialist bookkeeper who may not be full-time but will be able to write your books up for you as required. The accountant should be asked to advise on the way in which this is done; recommending account books, column headings and so on.

Such a member of staff, who may also have other duties, will qualify for the ancillary staff refund; this would not be the case with your accountancy fees.

▲ Question 109: Sources of information

I would like to find out much more about my accounts and how they work, together with some idea of finances for GPs in general. Where could I find out this information?

First, try and ensure that your practice has a fully up-to-date and amended copy of the Statement of Fees and Allowances (Red Book). This is an invaluable source of information on GP finances. The monthly *Medeconomics* also includes useful statistics and guidance, as does the weekly newspaper *Doctor* and *Financial Pulse*.

You should make a point of reading the regular articles that appear in medical journals.

The Institute of Chartered Accountants (Accountancy Books, Tel: 0171 833 3291) publishes a book entitled *Doctors' Accounts*, which gives much useful advice, specimen sets of accounts and many other items, although it is written for and aimed at the accountancy profession.

Making Sense of Practice Finance, published by Radcliffe Medical Press (Tel: 01235 528820), includes several chapters showing how practice accounts should be prepared and interpreted.

Finally, your own accountant should be willing to visit the partnership to talk through the practice accounts and explain them to you.

14

Practice Accounts

▲ Question 110: Can I do it myself?

My practice has an accountant and we think he is rather expensive. Indeed, we are thinking of terminating his services and saving his fees by doing it ourselves. Can we do this and do we really need accounts prepared to such a high standard?

There are really two points to this question. Firstly, there is nothing whatever in law that requires you to engage a professional accountant to act for you. Inspectors of Taxes will negotiate directly with taxpayers and there is no other authority that requires you to have accounts prepared to professional standards.

However, you may find it difficult if either the practice or the individual partners themselves seek to borrow money for any substantial amount, such as surgery improvement or extensions and house mortgages for the partners.

Whether the partners are able and willing to do the work is another matter. The work in preparing a set of accounts, even to such a basic level as would be acceptable to an Inspector of Taxes, is time-consuming and assumes the keeping of adequate accounting records. It also requires the application of a high level of accounting and taxation skill and knowledge. It may make better financial sense to pay a specialist accountant to deal with your accounts and tax, leaving the doctors the time to increase their earnings from practising medicine.

There is much valuable management information to be obtained from a properly drawn-up set of accounts.

Before taking any decision you should consult your partnership deed, which is likely to provide for accounts to be drawn up each year by a recognized firm of accountants.

▲ Question 111: Time taken to produce accounts

My partnership makes up its accounts to 31 December each year. The accountants normally start work on preparing our accounts shortly afterwards but in the last few years it has been well over a year since then that we have received a copy of the accounts. Is this too slow? What time should normally be taken by an accountant to produce these figures?

It is indeed inordinately slow. There is no apparent reason why your accounts should be as late as this unless your books and papers are in a state that will require a great deal of additional work by the accountant.

It would be a good idea to discuss this with your accountant, express your concern and enquire whether the process cannot be speeded up.

If you cannot get any satisfaction on this matter, it may be that you should consider changing your accountant because figures presented as late as this, apart from providing your figures upon which your tax assessment is based, are really of very little value to you in managing your practice.

It is difficult to lay down hard-and-fast guidelines, without taking into account all manner of other factors, such as the efficiency with which you produce information for the accountant. However, assuming that such factors do not apply, it would be not unreasonable to expect your accountant to supply you with a set of accounts for approval no later than 6 months after your accounting year-end or 3 months after putting the work in hand.

▲ Question 112: Accounting year-ends

I am setting up a new medical practice. To what year-end should I make up my accounts annually?

For some years accountants advised GPs to make up their accounts to 30 June, being the first quarter end within a fiscal year. With the coming of the current year basis of assessment, however, this has now changed and many small businesses will opt to make their accounts up to 31 March annually. Indeed, some established practices may well seek to change their accounts to that year-end, provided this causes no detriment in terms of tax payable.

▲ Question 113: Access to partnership accounts

I have just joined a medical practice and am horrified to find that I am not allowed to see copies of the partnership accounts. These are sent to our senior partner direct by the accountant and he will not show them to his partners. I would like to know how much I am earning. What can I do about it?

This really is a most unacceptable situation. If you are a member of the partnership in every sense of the word, you are fully entitled to see a copy of the accounts, indeed this should be included as a clause in your partnership deed (*see* Question 34). Furthermore, the accounts should be signed and approved by all the partners.

If the partnership accountant is also your own personal accountant you have a right to expect him to send these accounts to you as he should have your interests at heart. If you have engaged your own accountant, I suggest you ask him to write to the partnership accountant for a copy of the accounts.

Apart from this, I suggest you and your partners formally ask your senior partner to let you see a copy of the accounts, and that you should all instruct your accountant in writing to send final copies of them to your home addresses on completion. This is the manner by which most reputable accountants would circulate accounts to clients in partnership. Their role is to act for all the partners in the practice, not merely the senior partner.

▲ Question 114: Changes in partnership

Our partnership has changed much in the last few years, with several partners retiring and leaving and new ones joining. This has caused great difficulty to our accountant, who does not seem to understand how partnerships work, and we have been saddled with large amounts of tax arrears. How do we go about resolving this?

Certainly, the accountant should understand the dynamic nature of many GP partnerships, and that these can and do change at fairly frequent intervals. He should be able to advise you on items such as profit-sharing ratios, look through partnership deeds, submission of continuation elections and so on. The means by which partnership changes are accounted for are extremely complex, particularly concerning the allocation of income tax assessments (*see* Question 25), but your accountant should be conversant with these and be able to deal with re-allocations of tax liabilities, as and when they arise, without undue difficulty.

▲ Question 115: Capital accounts

I see the term 'capital accounts' in my practice's annual accounts and have been asked to contribute some capital into the practice. I do not understand this and cannot see why I should have to pay money to my partners. Nobody told me about this when I joined.

All medical practices are businesses, in exactly the same way as a corner shop or a public limited company; it is all a question of scale. Any business has to run on an injection of capital, which has to be originated from an agreed source. In the case of a limited company this will come from the investment by shareholders in the shares of that company. In a partnership there are no shareholders, the owners effectively being the partners in the practice and it is from these partners that the investment must come. In return for such an investment, they own their equivalent share of the capital of the practice and should be expected to contribute towards this accordingly. It would normally be set out in a partnership deed exactly how such capital is to be defined and calculated, and the fact that the partners are required to contribute this in their profit-sharing ratios.

The capital of a practice at any balance sheet date may well look something like Figure 7 (*see* page 118), which shows the figures for a dispensing practice.

	£	£
Fixed assets		15 000
Current assets:		
Stock on hand	10 000	
Sundry debtors	15 000	
Cash on hand	8 000	
	33 000	
Less: Sundry creditors	6 000	
		27 000
Net assets		42 000

Figure 7: Example of a balance sheet showing the capital in a practice.

It would be reasonable for a partner joining a practice on, say, an initial share of the profits of 10% to contribute an amount of £4200 (that is 10% of £42 000) and this can be realized from whatever source is available to him (*see* Question 27). Such a partner who was rising to parity within, say 3 years, would be expected to contribute a small amount appropriate to his rise in ratio each year so that when he achieves parity he owns a share of the capital equivalent to those of his partners.

▲ Question 116: Property capital accounts

What is the meaning of the term 'property capital'? In my practice, we own the surgery and I heard the term used by my partners and our accountant but do not understand what it means. I own a fifth share of our surgery.

In a surgery-owning partnership, it is essential that the investment of the surgery-owning partners is kept distinct from that of other partners. It is by no means uncommon for a partnership of, say, six doctors to have four of them owning the surgery, while the other two, possibly a partially retired partner and a part-time doctor, do not wish to invest in the premises. In such a case, those four partners would own the equity of the surgery, which could be calculated as shown in Figure 8.

	£
Book value of the surgery	400 000
Outstanding mortgage	300 000
Equity	100 000
One-quarter share	25 000

Figure 8: Example of a one-quarter share in the equity of the surgery.

In such a case, it is normal for this to be shown within the accounts by the creation of 'property capital' accounts, which would show those four doctors each owning a share with a value of £25 000. It follows that those partners only will share in the cost or notional rent allowances, which derive from the ownership of that surgery but will also be solely responsible for the capital and interest payments on the surgery mortgage.

Such a surgery is owned only by those partners and is nothing whatever to do with the partners who have not made such an investment. When such a property-owning partner retires, he or she can reasonably expect to be paid a share of such an ownership (*see* Question 40).

▲ Question 117: Property values

I own a share in my surgery premises and will be retiring shortly. I would like to obtain a proper valuation of the property and am not sure how to go about this. I have asked our accountant but he has declined to do so.

Your accountant is quite right – his professional skills do not include the valuation of properties and you should approach a valuer who is experienced and skilled in dealing with the valuation of doctors' surgeries. These should properly be valued on the basis of the building in use as a medical practice. You cannot therefore place a value upon it as if it were a residential property or a block of business offices.

Please try to ensure that all the partners are in agreement in principle before you go ahead. It is by no means uncommon to find a valuer placing a value upon a property to which the partners do not feel able to agree. This can cause dissension in partnerships and unnecessary expense when additional valuers have to be appointed. The agreed basis of valuation should be included in your partnership deed to avoid any uncertainty.

▲ Question 118: Treatment of leave advances

On looking at our practice accounts I can see no reference to the leave advance, which all the partners draw every year. On asking my accountant he seemed to be unaware of it, but told me that it is merely included with the rest of the fees and allowances. I do not think this is right. How should it be shown in the accounts?

There are a number of ways of showing the leave advance in the accounts, but what should most certainly not occur is that it is included as an item of income. This most certainly it is not; it is, to all intents and purposes, a loan to the partners involved for one year, and should be shown as such. It is not an item of income and the partners should not be asked to pay tax on it.

The most usual method of showing the leave advance in the accounts is merely to credit it to the partners' current accounts as an item of receipt, but then to show the leave advance repayments (which are deducted from the quarterly NHS fees and allowances) as an item of outgoing from the same current accounts. If the practice has a year-end of 31 March, which coincides with the NHS accounting year, this will have no difference whatever as the repayments will equal the advance. If, however, the practice uses an alternative year-end, the outgoings will be slightly different from the advance, and it is important that it is properly shown.

It is equally wrong to omit any reference to the leave advance. The annual accounts should reflect the financial transactions of the practice in any given year, and it should be evident from the accounts which of the partners received the leave advance during the same period.

▲ Question 119: Accruals: basis of accounts

Can you explain to me why my accountant asks at each year-end for details of monies owing to the practice and items that we owe to outsiders? Surely if these are paid the following year they should go in next year's accounts.

This is not strictly speaking the case. Very few practices still prepare accounts on a receipts and payments basis, which means that they account in a single year of account only for items for which cash is actually received and paid out during that year.

It is statistically unlikely that your practice will prepare its accounts on that basis. More likely it will prepare an account each year (called an income and expenditure account, or, rather less likely, a profit and loss account) which, as the name implies, shows, as exactly as possible, the amounts earned and expended during each year. For example, if you make up your accounts to 30 June annually and you receive a telephone bill on 28 June, under the accruals concept you would bring that item in as a creditor to the accounts on 30 June following. By this means the accounts would show the actual amount expended during the year by the practice, rather than merely payments made. This is why your accountant asks you for this information; he would be unable to prepare accurate accounts without it.

By this means it is necessary for there to be calculated, either by the practice or by the accountant, all amounts outstanding at each year-end. Let us take, for example, amounts earned from service fees. It is highly likely that such fees will be received well after the date they were actually earned, and many accountants treat these as being received a quarter in arrear. The calculation of these fees to be shown in an account for the year ended 30 June 1998 may well therefore be as follows:

	£
Actually received during year:	24 890
Add: Debtor (accrual) @ 30 June 1998	3 840
	28 730
Less: Debtor @ 1 July 1997	1 490
	27 240

It will be seen that, while the amounts earned by this practice from service fees during the year were £27 240, the actual amount received was £24 890 – very much lower.

It is right and proper therefore, firstly for the purpose of ensuring the tax liabilities are accurate, but also for making sure that partners receive their correct shares of profit, that a calculation of this type is made.

▲ Question 120: Partnerships: treatment of target payments

When I looked at my partnership accounts I saw that there was no income from target payments. This cannot surely be right? We have always hit our targets, or very nearly so, and we are most certainly due to some income from this source.

On enquiry from the accountants who drew up the accounts in the HA, I understand that this income came in after the year-end, but surely it is wrong not to show it in the accounts.

Indeed it is wrong not to show it as such. The accounts produced for you almost certainly will reflect the income and expenditure for the year, not the receipts and payments (*see* Question 119). What this means is that, so far as income is concerned, the accounts should reflect the amount actually earned in the year and not money actually received, which could well be rather different. To take an example, if a practice earned a fee of £50 on 25 June and it makes up its accounts to 30 June annually, that fee should be included in those accounts, despite the fact that the cheque was not received until, say, 15 July.

In an instance such as the one you have quoted, this could give rise to all manner of unfairness, particularly resulting from changes in profit-sharing ratios, where it is necessary to see that partners receive the correct share of the income to which they are entitled.

▲ Question 121: Adjustments to partners' balances

We are continually being recommended by our accountant either to make differential drawings at the end of each year or to refund money to the practice. I find this extremely disturbing, not to say at times expensive. Is this really necessary and how can we avoid it?

What I believe you are talking about is the process for equalization of your current account balances at the end of each year. Capital of this nature should ideally be contributed in profit-sharing ratios (*see* Question 27). In effect, such is the complexity of many of the transactions passing through the typical medical partnership that it is virtually impossible to calculate the partners' drawings so accurately that these current account balances at the end of each year are exactly equal. To a large degree the accuracy with which the drawings are calculated (*see* Question 36) is a direct reflection on the final current account balances of the partners at the end of the year. Your accountant is perfectly right in inviting you to equalize these; if this is not done methodically each year you will find that a 'snowball' effect arises so that the discrepancy between partners' balances magnifies each year until it becomes unmanageable. It is essential therefore that such a balancing process is done annually without fail.

Ideally, the capital of the partnership (*see* Question 27) should be properly organized so that the partners are each able to withdraw the balance on their respective current accounts at the end of each year. This, however, assumes that each partner has contributed adequate funds to cover his capital requirements.

Your partnership deed is likely to lay down exactly what procedures are to be taken in the event of partners becoming overdrawn on their current accounts, but it is inevitably better if the practice finances are organized in such an efficient manner that this situation does not arise.

▲ Question 122: 'Grossing-up'

We practise in a health centre and I have asked our accountant to show, on both sides of the accounts, the rent and rates figures for the health centre.

He will not do so and says he does not understand why it should be done. How can we solve this?

It is essential that, for the purposes of the annual review body award, such notional rent and rates figures on your health centre accommodation are entered on both sides of your accounts. The figure of rent and rates should be shown as a payment and the notional refund as an item of income. This will have no effect whatsoever on your final profit or your tax position but it serves to maximize the level of expenses in case those accounts are ever used by the review body in their process of calculating the doctors' pay award each year. This is emphasized regularly by the BMA and the authority for this is contained in paragraph 53.4 of the Statement of Fees and Allowances (Red Book).

This 'grossing-up' principle does not only apply to notional health centre charges but to all other items for which direct refunds are obtained, such as actual rent and rates payments, ancillary staff salaries, drug refunds, training salaries and so on.

Your accountant should be instructed that he is to prepare the accounts accordingly. Failure to do so can severely affect the level of the GPs' pay awards each year and it is in the interests of yourself and the profession as a whole that this should be done.

The figures should be provided to you on a regular basis by your Health Authority and if this is not done you should take steps to see that they are obtained and passed on to your accountant for completing your accounts. If he still declines to do so it is suggested that a change might be in order and that you should engage a more specialist firm (*see* Question 107) who will understand why it is so important to draw up the accounts in the prescribed manner.

▲ Question 123: Cash flow

I recently attended a meeting where my practice was recommended to take advice regarding our cash flow. I cannot see why we should do so: surely we know exactly how much is coming into and out of the practice and there is little we can do to control this. Should I pay to have this done, if at all, or should we try to do it ourselves?

A cash-flow statement is essential for the good financial administration of any medical practice, or indeed any other business. The advantages you would derive from this are that you could have greater control over the funds passing through the practice and be able to ensure that the bank account does not become overdrawn, thus running up bank charges and interest on overdrafts.

This system does not replace the ordinary routine system of bookkeeping, which the practice should maintain (*see* Questions 2, 3 and 4). Many cash-flow predictions are prepared on a monthly basis using a standard computer program. Such a cash-flow statement can also be used for preparing budgets and giving the partners an idea how much they are likely to be able to take from the practice in the form of drawings. They will also be useful, and may be requested by your bank, if you seek loan finance for any reason.

If properly used, such a cash-flow system can be of great benefit to the practice. It need not necessarily be prepared by an outside accountant, although this could be done if you wish. Many practices prepare their own cash-flow statements, probably for a year hence at any given date and these should be updated and corrected when actual figures for any particular month are available.

Figure 9 is a schedule that gives a brief outline of such a cash-flow forecast. It will be seen that the partners' drawings do not vary to any great degree and the practice shown may be well advised, when there are months during which the bank account is likely to become overdrawn, to reduce the partners' drawings to avoid this happening. It is possible to make such predictions by the use of cash-flow forecasts. They can also highlight months in which the practice is likely to have surplus funds available, and this can be useful when future capital outlay on new equipment is being considered.

Practice accounts • 127

	April	May	June	July	Aug	Sept	Oct	Nov	Dec	Jan	Feb	March	TOTAL
Receipts													
NHS Fees/Allowances	9 500	9 500	11 365	9 800	9 800	13 652	9 800	9 800	12 653	10 000	10 000	13 652	129 522
Ancillary staff	438	1 294	1 066	1 003	1 070	1 107	856	908	927	927	998	1 080	11 673
Trainee refunds	640	640	640	720	720	720	720	845	845	845	845	845	9 025
Rent and rates	750	750	750	2 975	750	750	750	750	750	750	750	750	11 225
Drugs refunds	0	0	0	192	0	0	70	190	1 296	0	16	0	1 764
Insurance exams	300	78	250	220	443	401	249	419	426	777	215	312	4 090
Cremation fees	21	0	21	0	23	42	0	0	42	21	0	0	170
Appointments	208	208	208	208	208	208	208	208	208	208	208	208	2 496
Sundry fees	62	42	163	0	0	315	27	63	0	412	0	0	1 084
TOTAL INCOME	11 919	12 512	14 463	15 118	13 014	17 195	12 680	13 183	17 147	13 940	13 032	16 847	171 049

Figure 9: Practice cash-flow forecast.

continued overleaf

128 • Practice Finance: your questions answered

	April	May	June	July	Aug	Sept	Oct	Nov	Dec	Jan	Feb	March	TOTAL
Payments													
Staff salaries and NIC	617	1822	1 502	1412	1507	1559	1206	1279	1305	1305	1406	1521	16 441
Trainee salaries	640	640	640	720	720	720	720	845	845	845	845	845	9 025
Locum fees	432	512	245	0	315	645	315	545	215	150	450	215	4 039
Relief service fees	70	35	0	70	75	40	62	52	120	0	0	75	599
Drugs and instruments	172	0	0	56	200	1300	0	20	0	0	42	23	1 813
Rent and rates	750	750	3 725	750	750	750	750	750	750	750	750	750	11 975
Repairs and renewals	72	0	84	12	160	0	0	51	20	0	0	61	460
Petty cash	100	100	100	100	100	100	100	100	100	200	100	100	1 300
Loan interest	423	389	532	423	398	452	396	401	463	363	431	462	5 133
Loan repayments	500	500	500	500	500	500	500	500	500	500	500	500	6 000
Accountancy fees	0	1500	262	0	500	352	300	0	123	0	0	273	3 310
Insurance	0	0	0	0	0	750	0	0	0	840	0	0	1 590
Lighting and heating	0	98	0	55	46	0	0	62	59	0	0	0	320
Bank charges and interest	0	0	96	0	0	162	0	0	73	0	0	106	437
Telephone	0	0	839	0	0	433	0	0	926	0	0	519	2 717
Drawings	7500	7500	12 636	7900	7900	7900	7900	7900	7900	7900	7900	7900	98 736
Sundries	72	0	735	42	78	24	924	0	0	2460	260	107	4 702
NET CASH FLOW	571	−1334	−7 433	3078	−235	1508	−493	678	3748	−1373	348	3390	2 452
Opening bank balance	1604	2175	841	−6 592	−3514	−3749	−2242	−2734	−2056	1691	318	666	1 604
Closing bank balance	2175	841	−6 592	−3514	−3749	−2242	−2734	−2056	1691	318	666	4056	4 056

Figure 9: continued

15

GP Fundholding

GP fundholding is, we are told, to end on 31 March 1999. The questions in this chapter are, therefore, of limited currency and should be considered in that light.

▲ Question 124: Professional assistance

We are a practice with four partners and 9000 patients. Unfortunately, we find the accounting extremely difficult to understand and my staff have problems in understanding the computer program we were given. Is there any help I can obtain? Can I pay an accountant to assist us?

There are several sources of help you can obtain. All the companies supplying computer software run telephone helplines from which you should be able to obtain immediate help as required. Your HA will have access to sources of information which again will enable them to clarify the accounting system. Regular training courses are organized on fundholding accountancy and are advertised regularly in the specialist journals.

You can, if you wish, pay an outside accountant to help you with your accounts. His fees will be charged to you on the basis of the work he performs and you would expect to pay them out of the management allowance, provided of course that you have not fully spent the amount of the allowance. Subject to this, there is no reason why this cost should not fall on the management allowance.

In the earlier years of fundholding, some practices did indeed seek outside professional assistance in helping them with their accounts. As time has moved on, however, many of those practices have now engaged the services of qualified and experienced project managers, who are perfectly capable of dealing with the accountancy side of their fundholding facility, and it is suggested that it may well be more economical for you to seek help from your own staff than to rely on outside assistance on a regular basis.

▲ Question 125: Audit of accounts

We shall shortly be nearing the end of our first year as a fundholding practice. I understand that these accounts must be audited. Who will do the audit? Will it be our own practice accountants or outsiders?

The requirement for audit is that the accounts of the fundholding practice, which are separate and distinct from those of the general practice, must be audited once a year. The original intention was that these would be audited at triennial intervals by accountants working for the Audit Commission. What has happened so far for the first few waves of fundholding is that the Audit Commission have completed these audits for the first two years. After that it appears likely that internal audits will be conducted by the HA, with the Audit Commission dealing with the audit at three-year intervals.

Please bear in mind also that the Audit Commission have the right of access to your general practice accounts although it is unlikely that this right will be exercised, except in somewhat unusual circumstances.

Your own practice accountants will not normally have a role to play in this fundholding audit. There is no reason, if you are unsure of the accuracy of your accounts, you should not instruct your own or other accountants to review the accounts before the audit commences. Some practices feel they would prefer to do this to ensure their own peace of mind. In such circumstances, of course, a fee will be payable which would ideally be negotiated in advance.

▲ Question 126: Fundholding bank account

We are a practice new to fundholding and have been instructed to set up a separate bank account for the receipt and payment of monies forming part of the fund. What will this bank account contain and should we have it at the same branch as our own practice account?

Our accountant says that when we prepare our accounts, as this is in the name of the partners, we must show it as an asset in our balance sheet. Is this right?

You should indeed open a separate fundholding bank account, as specified in the Manual of Accounts. This account will be used predominantly for the receipt and payment of monies in connection with the ancillary staff part of your overall fund.

From time to time, normally monthly, the HA will pay you an amount in accordance with the budget, probably one-twelfth at the end of each month, in order to recompense you for this. From time to time you will make payments to the practice bank account in respect of your entitlement to this ancillary staff refund. The two amounts coming into the account and going out of it will not necessarily be the same.

The main difference here is, if you were not a fundholding practice, these amounts would be paid to you directly by the HA. Now that you are a fundholding practice, the refunds will be made, not direct from the HA, but from your fundholding bank account.

It must be emphasized that this account is not in the beneficial ownership of the partners. Any balance on it from time to time belongs to the HA and not to the practice. On no account must it be included in the overall figure of 'cash at bank and in hand', normally included in your balance sheet.

▲ Question 127: Bank interest and charges

We have, as we were instructed, set up a separate fundholding bank account into which we pay money received from the HA as part of our staff budget. The bank has debited bank charges and, occasionally, interest to this account. Should we get the HA to repay this to us, or does the cost fall on the practice?

Provided the fundholding bank account is kept at the same bank as your practice bank account, it is normally a good idea to ask the bank to make any charges on the fundholding account to the practice account. You should then claim these as part of your management allowance. Provided that you have not exceeded the maximum amount of the allowance to which you are entitled, then these charges should be repaid to you by the HA, so cancelling out the charge which has effectively been made against the practice.

▲ Question 128: Interest on fundholding bank account

As a fundholding practice, we retain in hand in a separate fundholding bank account small amounts of money which are received from the HA from time to time, largely to cover our staff budget. These monies are held in an interest-bearing account, which is credited with small amounts of interest from time to time. Can we retain this interest in the practice and does it have to be declared for tax purposes?

No, this interest does not belong to the partners or to the practice; it is generated from money which is not owned by the partners but is merely held by them 'on trust' for the HA. As such, the interest must be returned to the HA through the fundholding accounting system.

This interest, although it has borne tax at source, does not form part of the income of the practice and the partners should not show it on their own personal tax returns.

▲ Question 129: Fund savings: how to spend them

It seems clear that our first year's budget will show an underspend and there will be money available to spend on the practice. How can we use this money?

Some of the partners feel that they would like new cars with which to conduct the practice business and I wonder if the savings can be used for this purpose?

Firstly, the doctors would be well advised to accept that under no circumstances whatever will they be allowed to buy private cars out of fund savings. Most HAs would decline to accept that this was expenditure for the good of the patients and the doctors would be well advised to forget this one.

Fund savings have been successfully used for the purchase of all manner of equipment for use in the surgery: X-ray machines, heart machines, and the like. Some practices have bought mini-buses to bring patients from outlying areas and savings have been used to finance the extension and improvement of surgery premises.

Any fund savings of this sort cannot be spent without the explicit approval of the HA, who will also be responsible for actually paying the bill for purchase of any such equipment.

▲ Question 130: Fund savings: ownership by partners

We are a five-doctor practice and joined the fundholding scheme in the first wave in 1991. Since then, we have been able to acquire assets of the practice out of our fund savings. Our senior partner has now told us that he intends to retire from the practice in a year's time and that he expects us to buy from him his share of the practice assets, some of which were purchased through fund savings. As the partners have never actually paid any of their own money for these assets, is it right that we should have to pay him for them?

The outgoing partner in such circumstances is perfectly within his rights in insisting on payment for these assets. It is clearly laid down in the Manual of Accounts that these assets are in the beneficial ownership of the partners and they have every right to sell them to the partners on leaving the practice.

Whether this is correct or morally fair must be left to your combined judgement; in the event of you being unable to reach any other agreement, then there is no doubt that any such share of assets must be paid to the outgoing partner.

In some circumstances, those practices who have been aware of the situation have sought to correct this by agreeing amongst themselves that assets bought either in this manner or out of the fundholding management allowance will be treated as 'community property' and it be agreed that these be retained in the surgery for the use of the patients and the practice in perpetuity. If practices wish to go down this road, then it is essential that a form of agreement be signed between them. This should be accepted by all the partners in the practice from time to time and a clear inventory should be kept identifying any assets acquired by this means.

▲ Question 131: Surplus invested in surgery

We are using our fundholding savings to refurbish the surgery premises. The premises are owned by five of the seven existing partners. The partners who share in the ownership of the property stand to benefit from the refurbishment due to the enhancement in the value of the property. How can we ensure that the non-property-owning partners are fairly treated?

There can surely be no better argument for maintaining a policy that all GPs own equivalent shares in their surgery premises. However, this is not the case here. Quite clearly, any such surplus belongs to all the partners in the practice and it is inequitable that they should not all share in it. The best practical solution would be for the non-surgery-owning partners to buy into the building at the earliest opportunity. However, there may well be abiding reasons why they do not choose to do so.

The only alternative could be that the property-owning partners compensate the non-surgery owners in some mutually agreeable manner, although even this course of action would be fraught with potential problems. For example, and particularly on the introduction of new partners, such transactions could be construed as a sale of goodwill, which is illegal under the NHS Acts. It may be possible to compensate these partners through a policy of making cash gifts, but even there, Inheritance Tax implications arise which should be discussed with the practice accountant.

▲ Question 132: Savings in ancillary staff costs

When we entered into the fundholding scheme we negotiated with our HA an allowance for part of the fund which covered our ancillary staff costs. We understood at the time, that if we made any saving on this we could retain the money, in the same way as savings can be retained in respect of the hospital services' prescribing budgets. The HA is now asking us to return the money to them but we do not think this is correct.

It does seem that in some cases HAs have sought to have this money returned, rather than being dealt with as part of an overall saving on the total budget.

If you make a saving on the staff budget then the policy of 'virement' comes into play and you can either set the saving against overspends on other components of the budget or, in the case of an overspend, then this must be recovered from savings elsewhere in the fund. Any overall saving would merely be dealt with as part of the fund saving (*see* Question 129).

▲ Question 133: GP fundholding taxation

We are a large fundholding practice with a total agreed budget of £1.6m. So far as I can calculate, it seems that we shall, in the present year, spend only about £1.4m of this, giving us a saving of £200 000. Will we have to pay tax on this? If we buy any equipment out of these savings, will this be taxable?

You can rest safely in the knowledge that fund savings are not taxable. The Inland Revenue have agreed that the fund itself, not being in the beneficial ownership of the partners, is not part of their income and hence not taxable. By the same token of course, you cannot receive relief on any expenses you pay out of your fund, such as hospital or drug costs.

No money in fact is allocated to the practice until such time as the HA have agreed that money can be spent out of this saving. If you purchase an asset out of this, then you have acquired this asset at no cost to the practice and will be unable to claim capital allowances for tax purposes in the same way as if you had bought an asset out of your free capital.

If you spend money out of fund savings to cover some revenue cost, such as the decoration of the surgery, in theory this would then be the taxable income of the practice, although this would, of course, be fully offset by the cost of the re-decoration which is a perfectly legitimate charge in your accounts.

Index

abatement of pension 87–8
accountants
  bookkeeping 111
  changing 109–10
  fees 108
  finding 110–11
  partnership 107
  personal 107
accounting records 2–3
  computerized 4
accounts 23
  accruals 121–2
  allowances 9
  bank accounts *see* bank accounts
  bookkeeping 3–4
  capital accounts 117–18
  cash 7–8
  cash flow 125–6, *127–8*
  debtors 13–14
  drawings calculations 10–11, *12*
  gifts to staff 14–15
  grossing-up 124–5
  information sources 112
  leave advances 8, 120–1
  partners' access to 115–16
  partners' balances 123–4
  partnership changes 116–17
  petty cash 7–8
  practice management 1–2
  property capital accounts 118–19
  property values 119–20
  self-preparation 113–14
  staffing budgets 15–16
  stock on hand 11–13
  target payments 123
  time taken to produce 114–15
  year ends 115
accruals 121–2
added years superannuation 90, 92
additional income, new partners 34–5
AISMA (Association of Independent Specialist Medical Accountants) 111
allowances available, new partners 34

Association of Independent Specialist Medical Accountants (AISMA) 111
Audit Commission 130
audit of accounts, fundholding 130

bank accounts
  balancing 5–6
  fundholding 131–2
    interest and charges 132
    interest received 132–3
  reconciliation statements 6
basic practice allowance (BPA)
  leave advances 8
  new partners 34
BMA Professional Services Ltd 111
bookkeepers 2, 3, 4
bookkeeping 3–4, 111
BPA *see* basic practice allowance

capital 124
  accounts 117–18
  finance for introduction 32
  introduction of 31–2
capital allowances
  cars 67–8, 69, 70, 71
  fundholding 137
Capital Gains Tax (CGT)
  annual exemption 75, 101
  house
    sales 75, 78
    use of 62
  indexation relief 74
  land sales 77–8
  re-basing 74–5
  retirement relief 45–6, 52, 54, 78
  roll-over relief 78
  share sales 74–5
  surgery premises 45–6, 52, 54
cars
  capital allowances 67–8, 69, 70, 71

expensive 70, 71
financing purchase 68
leasing 69
mileage logs 72–3, 73
time to purchase 67–8
trainees' allowances 27–8, 70–2
cash 7–8
cash flow 125–6, *127–8*
CGT *see* Capital Gains Tax
changing accountants 108–10
children
  child minding 60
  investments for 100
Christmas gifts to staff 14–15
Christmas parties for staff 15
clothing 64–5
computerized accounting records 4
conference expenses 62–3
cost-rent *see* surgery premises
current account balances 123–4
current year basis, income tax 24

de-merger of partnerships 39
debtors 13–14
Deeds of Family Arrangement 104
demands, income tax 19–20
dispensations, income tax 28, 70
dispensing practices
  drug refunds as debtors 13
  stock on hand valuation 11–13
  Value Added Tax registration 56
drawings
  calculations 10–11, *12*
  income tax and 39–40
drug refunds, as debtors 13
duality of purpose 59–60

employees *see* staff
endowment policies 103, 105–6
examination fees 63

Index • 141

expenses *see* personal practice expenses; practice expenses
expensive cars 70, *71*

Family Arrangement, Deeds of 104
fees
  accountants' 108
  item of service fees as debtors 13
  unrecorded 7
finance
  for capital introduction, new partners 32
  for car purchase 68
  new premises 53–4
financial management 1–16
Free-Standing Additional Voluntary Contributions (FSAVC) 98–9
fundholding *see* GP fundholding

gifts
  in kind 15
  to staff 14–15
GP fundholding
  audit of accounts 130–1
  bank accounts 131–2
    interest and charges 132
    interest received 132–3
  fund savings
    in ancillary staff costs 136
    ownership by partners 134–5
    spending 133–4
    surgery refurbishment 135
  professional assistance 129–30
  taxation 136–7
grossing-up 124–5

health centres 48–50, 124–5
health promotion payments, as debtors 13–14
holidays
  leave advances 8, 120–1

houses
  claims for use of 61–2
  land adjoining, sale 77–8
  mortgage interest relief 65–6
  sales, Capital Gains Tax 75, 78
  use of, Capital Gains Tax 62
husbands' salaries 82–3

IHT *see* Inheritance Tax
income tax
  current year basis 24
  demands 19–20
  dispensations 28, 70
  drawings and 39–40
  fundholding 136–7
  gifts to staff 14–15
  interest
    on overdue tax 20
    on repayments 21, 22
  married couple's allowance 79–80
    in year of marriage 86
  notional rent allowances 47
  overdue, interest on 20
  in partnerships 29–30
  penalties 26–7
  pensions 93–4
  preceding year basis 24
  repayments
    allocation to partners 21–2
    interest on 21, 22
    repayment supplement 21, 22
  retirement tax position 94–5
  returns 23
    non-submission penalties 26–7
  self-assessment *see* self-assessment
  superannuation
    allowances 88–9
    relief renunciation 92–3
  trainee car allowances 27–8, 70–2
  in year of marriage 86
indexation relief 74

Inheritance Tax (IHT) 76
  exemptions 103–4
  fundholding savings 135
  surviving spouse exemption 77
interest paid
  on finance for capital introduction 32
  fundholding accounts 132
  on overdue income tax 20
  on repayments income tax 21, 22
interest received
  fundholding accounts 132–3
investments
  Capital Gains Tax exemption 101
  for children 100
  endowment policies 103, 105–6
  Inheritance Tax exemptions 103–4
  life assurance 105–6
  mid-term endowment policies 103
  National Savings 100, 101, 104–5
  Personal Equity Plans (PEP) 102
  Premium Savings Bonds 105
  Tax-Exempt Special Savings Accounts (TESSA) 101
  tax-free 101
item of service fees, as debtors 13

land sales 77–8
leasing cars 69
leave advances 8, 120–1
life assurance 103, 105–6
locum insurance 66
lump-sum pension payments 93

married couple's allowance *see* income tax
married women doctors
  husbands' salaries 82–3
medical insurance policies 66, 85–6
mid-term endowment policies 103

mileage logs 72–3, 73
mortgage interest relief 65–6

National Insurance contributions (NIC)
  Class 1 18, 70, 80
  Class 2 17–18
  Class 4 18
  gifts to staff 14–15
  recovery 16, 18
National Savings 100, 101, 104–5
negative equity 43–4
new partners *see* partnerships
new surgeries *see* surgery premises
NHS incomes
  as debtors 13
NIC *see* National Insurance contributions
notional rent allowances *see* surgery premises

out of hours work, medical earnings 36
overdue income tax, interest on 20
overseas conference expenses 62–3

parity, progress to 33–4, 118
partial exemption scheme, VAT 56–7
Partnership Act 1890 38
partnership deeds
  accounting records 3
  need for 38–9
  postgraduate education allowances (PGEA) 9
  seniority allowances 9
partnerships
  access to accounts 115–16
  accounts *see* accounts
  accumulation of earnings 37
  capital 124
    accounts 117–18
    introduction of 31–2
  changes, accounting for 116–17
  current account balances 123–4

de-merger 39
deeds *see* partnership deeds
drawings 39–40
expenses 58–9
fundholding savings, ownership 134–5
funds, realization on retirement 95
income tax *see* income tax
new partners
  additional income 34–5
  allowances available 34
  capital, introduction of 31–2
  finance for capital introduction 32
  parity, progress to 33–4
out of hours work, medical earnings 36
parity, progress to 33–4, 118
personal practice expenses 23, 58–9
profit allocations 30–1
rent allowances, allocation 48
retirement, relief for expenses 32–3
self-assessment 25–6
seniority awards 35–6
superannuation 35–6
surgery premises *see* surgery premises
taxation and drawings 39–40
wives' salaries 83–4
penalties, income tax 26–7
pensions
  abatement 87–8
  Free-Standing Additional Voluntary Contributions (FSAVC) 98–9
  lump-sum payments 93
  private contributions 91–2
    renunciation of NHS tax relief 92
    opting out of NHS superannuation scheme 96–7
  taxation 93–4
  wives 84–5
  see also retirement; superannuation
PEP (Personal Equity Plans) 102

permanent health insurance 66
Personal Equity Plans (PEP) 102
personal pension contributions *see* private pension contributions
personal practice expenses 58–9
  annual claims for 23
personal tax allowances
  married couple's allowance *see* income tax: married couple's allowance
personal taxpayers
  self-assessment 25
PET (potentially-exempt transfers) 104
petty cash 7–8
postgraduate education allowances (PGEA) 9, 35
  new partners 34
potentially-exempt transfers (PET) 104
practice accounts *see* accounts
practice expenses
  child minding 60
  clothing 64–5
  conference expenses 62–3
  duality of purpose 59–60
  examination fees 63
  house
    claims for use of 61–2
    mortgage interest relief 65–6
  locum insurance 66
  in partnerships 58–9
  permanent health insurance 66
  sickness insurance premiums 66
  video recorders 64
practice management 1–2
preceding year basis, income tax 24
premises *see* surgery premises
Premium Savings Bonds 105
private houses *see* houses
private pension contributions 91–2
  renunciation of NHS tax relief 92
  opting out of NHS superannuation scheme 96–7

profit allocations 30–1
property capital accounts 118–19

rates, health centres 48–50, 124–5
re-basing 74–5
receipts, sundry 7
Red Book (Statement of Fees and Allowances) 112
rent
  cost-rent *see* surgery premises
  health centres 48–50, 124–5
  non-surgery-owning partners 50
  notional allowances *see* surgery premises
repayment supplement, income tax 21, 22
retirement
  24-hour 87
  abatement of pension 87–8
  at age 50 95–6
  partnership funds, realization 95
  relief *see* Capital Gains Tax
  relief for expenses 32–3
  superannuation contributions after 88
  surgery premises considerations *see* surgery premises
  tax position 94–5
  see also pensions; superannuation
roll-over relief 78

salaries
  husbands 82–3
  staffing budgets 15–16
  wives 81–2, 83–4
self-assessment 3
  partnerships 25–6
  personal taxpayers 25
seniority awards 9, 35–6
share sales 74–5
sickness insurance premiums 66, 85–6

spouses
  husbands' salaries 82–3
  married couple's allowance *see* income tax
  medical insurance policies 85–6
  surviving, exemption 77
  wives
    outside employment 80–1
    pensions 84–5
    salaries 81–2, 83–4
staff
  ancillary cost savings 136
  Christmas parties for 15
  gifts to 14–15
  salaries 15–16
staffing budgets 15–16
Statement of Fees and Allowances (Red Book) 112
stock on hand, valuation 11–13
sundry receipts 7
superannuation 35–6
  added years 90, 92
  contributions after retirement 88
  opting out of NHS scheme 96–7
  tax allowances 88–9
  tax relief renunciation 92–3
  trainees' car allowances 70
  see also pensions; superannuation
surgery premises
  abatement of direct refunds 51
  cost-rent
    finance 53–4
    income 46
    Value Added Tax on new premises 55
  expenditure refunds 41–2
  fundholding savings invested in 135
  negative equity 43–4
  new
    finance for 53–4
    Value Added Tax 55

new partners' investments in 31
notional rent allowances
  allocation 48
  assessment 42
  tax treatment 47
property capital accounts
    118–19
rates, health centres 48–50
refurbishment through fundholding
    savings 135
rent
  health centres 48–50
  non-surgery-owning partners 50
retirement
  Capital Gains Tax 45–6, 52, 54
  income from ownership
      after 52–3
  negative equity 43–4
  sale of share 97–8
  sale proceeds 44–5, 45
  sole ownership 54
  valuations 119–20
  Value Added Tax 55
surviving spouse exemption 77

target payments 123
tax *see* Capital Gains Tax; income tax;
        Inheritance Tax; Value Added Tax
Tax-Exempt Special Savings Accounts
    (TESSA) 101
tax-free investments 101
trainees' car allowances
  income tax 27–8, 70–2
travelling *see* cars
24-hour retirement 87

unrecorded fees 7

valuations
  surgery premises 119–20
Value Added Tax
  car leasing 69
  on new premises 55
  partial exemption scheme 56–7
video recorders 64

wives *see* spouses

year ends 115